Ultimate Beginner's Guide to PRESERVING AND CANNING

Simple and Efficient Methods for Preserving, Pickling, and Making Jams with a Variety of Vegetables, Fruits, and Meats

THE EDITORS OF
THE HARVARD COMMON PRESS

NEW SHOE PRESS

Quarto.com

First Published in 2023 by New Shoe Press, an imprint of The Quarto Group,
100 Cummings Center, Suite 265-D, Beverly, MA 01915, USA.
T (978) 282-9590 F (978) 283-2742

Essential, In-Demand Topics, Four-Color Design, Affordable Price
New Shoe Press publishes affordable, beautifully designed books covering evergreen, in-demand subjects. With a goal to inform and inspire readers' everyday hobbies, from cooking and gardening to wellness and health to art and crafts, New Shoe titles offer the ultimate library of purposeful, how-to guidance aimed at meeting the unique needs of each reader. Reimagined and redesigned from Quarto's best-selling backlist, New Shoe books provide practical knowledge and opportunities for all DIY enthusiasts to enrich and enjoy their lives.

Visit Quarto.com/New-Shoe-Press for a complete listing of the New Show Press books.

New Shoe Press titles are also available at discount for retail, wholesale, promotional, and bulk purchase. For details, contact the Special Sales Manager by email at specialsales@quarto.com or by mail at The Quarto Group, Attn: Special Sales Manager, 100 Cummings Center, Suite 265-D, Beverly, MA 01915, USA.

ISBN: 978-0-7603-9530-1

The content in this book was previously published in *The Ultimate Guide to Preserving & Canning* (The Harvard Common Press 2020) by Lela Nargi, Ana Micka, Allison Carroll Duffy, and Amelia Jeanroy and *Preserving and Canning for Beginners* (New Shoe Press 2023).

Library of Congress Cataloging-in-Publication Data available

Photography: Glenn Scott Photography; except pages 27, 48, 50, 62, and 66 (Shutterstock)

The National Center for Home Food Preservation (NCHFP) website can be found at http://nchfp.uga.edu.

Printed in China

Contents

Chapter 1

Preserving the Best of the Harvest

Whether you are looking for the simple basics you need for getting started preserving and canning your harvest, or you're looking for invaluable advice for taking your canning to the next level, you'll find all the motivation and information you need in this chapter. You'll learn what equipment is essential to have on hand (and what is unnecessary), quick and easy precautions you can take to keep your treats safe and tasty, and troubleshooting tips that address all the common messy mistakes and storage conundrums awaiting every novice and veteran canner.

Water Bath Canning Vs. Pressure Canning

Water bath canning and pressure canning are similar in that they are both ways to preserve food in your own kitchen. The general process of putting food in jars, attaching lids, heating to seal, and storing are the same. However, there are some major differences you should know.

All foods have natural acidity levels. Many fruits and tomatoes are highly acidic. These foods can be water bath canned. Or, produce can be incorporated in a recipe that makes it safe for water bath canning, such as pickles: cucumbers (a low-acid food) are canned in an acidic pickling solution.

Water bath canning, or boiling water canning as it's sometimes called, is the method of submerging filled jars into hot water and boiling for a specific period of time. This means the internal temperature of the food in the jars is heated to 212°F (100°C). It's a great way to start canning and the most common way to make popular pantry items such as jams, jellies, and pickles. However, to get a wider range of foods in jars, you need to learn the art of pressure canning, which is discussed in detail in The Pressure Canning Process on page 32.

Pressure canning is the preserving method by which filled jars are placed into a large pot with just a few inches (7.5 to 10 cm) of water in it. A locking lid is placed on the pot and steam develops inside the pot. The jars' contents reach an internal temperature of 240°F (116°C) under a specific pressure (in pounds, see page 32), and the recipe states a specific period of time to hold that pressure. Pressure canning can be used for a wider variety of foods. You can process vegetables and fruits with low or high acidity, meats, poultry, fish, sauces, and even whole recipes—such as soups or stews. Pressure canning generally means less mess, and my jars always seem to seal when I pressure can. (I also admit some bias—I love canning meat. On the farm, we raise much of our own meat, and being able to process it myself means I can fill my pantry with healthy food that has been raised ethically.)

Pressure canning, as you might expect, is done in a *pressure canner*. A pressure canner is a large pot designed specifically for the canning process; do not confuse a pressure *canner* with a pressure *cooker*. A pressure cooker is very useful, but it's a different piece of equipment meant for general cooking. Although there is some crossover, and electric pressure cookers can be used to can a couple of jars at a time, they are two distinctly different kitchen items with similar names.

Canning Equipment

Canning is much easier and safer if you make use of the equipment readily available in your local hardware, farm, or home supply store or online. Jars, lids, and canning-specific ingredients like pectin are available at most grocery stores.

The Canner

The most important piece of equipment is the canner itself. The two types of canners available are boiling water bath canners and pressure canners.

Boiling Water Bath Canner. This type of canner consists of a large pot with a canning rack and a lid. Canning pots are usually 21 or 33 quarts (about 20 or 31 liters). You can use regular pots with lids as long as they are large enough to allow for at least 2 inches (5 cm) of water over the jars.

Pressure Canner. This type of canner consists of a large aluminum pot with a twist-on, locking lid, inner sealing rim, a rack, and a pressure gauge. The most popular pressure canner sizes are 16 or 22 quarts (about 15 or 21 liters). The smaller pressure cookers, usually 4-, 6-, or 8-quart (3.8, 5.7, or 7.6 liter) sizes, are great for daily cooking but are not approved for home canning. We will discuss pressure canners in depth in Pressure Canning Basics on page 26.

Essential Canning Equipment

Canning Rack. Most canners come with a canning rack. The rack for boiling water bath canners has slots for the jars and handles to lift the rack in and out of the canner. Pressure canners come with flat, plate-style racks that sit at the bottom of the canner. A rack protects the jars from direct heat on the bottom of the pan and prevents them from bouncing around during processing. Make sure to use a canning rack every time you can!

Jars: These come in a variety of sizes and your recipe will indicate the correct size for the food you are canning. Jars are typically sold by the dozen for the most common jar sizes, though higher-end, fancier jars may be sold individually. For more information on jars, see Let's Talk About Jars on page 29.

Jar Lids: The lid is critical to a well-sealed jar, not just for the covering you can see it provides but also for the seal it creates underneath. The most common type of canning jars and lids are the variety made by large manufacturers such as Ball. The lids have two pieces: the flat lid itself and a screw band that goes around the outside of the lid (see the next item in this list). If you look at the underside of one of these canning jar lids, you will see a reddish-brown ring around the edge. This ring softens during processing and forms an airtight seal as it cools. Jar lids with this sealing compound are *not* reusable; however, you can reuse the jars and screw bands. Just buy a new pack of lids before the next canning session.

Screw Bands: These bands are designed to hold the lid in place during processing. Since they can be reused, carefully inspect them for nicks, rust, and other signs the band has been weakened. As you'll read repeatedly in the recipes, the bands are screwed onto the jars until hand-tight, also called fingertip tight, and no tighter. They need to be loose enough to allow the jar lid to release air during processing. Screw bands can be removed after the jars cool completely to room temperature. Removing the band does not affect the lid seal and with no band to hide the seal it is easier to watch for any signs of leakage while the jar is in storage.

Canning Funnel: Use a canning funnel to fill your jars. You might think this would be an optional piece of equipment; however, keeping the rim of the jar clean is very important. Because you will be working with very hot foods and liquids, using a funnel will help keep your hands from getting burned as well. A canning funnel has a wide mouth and is wider than a normal funnel at the bottom to accommodate big pieces of food. They are inexpensive, and I recommend buying a few. I have both metal and plastic funnels in my canning supplies and both work equally well.

Electronic Scale: I recommend a digital scale that is reliable and that includes a tare function. (Tare means you can place your container on the scale and then set it back to 0 before weighing your ingredients.) I also prefer battery-powered scales so you don't have to deal with a cord.

Jar Lifter: This specialized item makes your canning experience much easier. You'll use the jar lifter to safely lift hot jars from the canner and protect your hands from hot water and steam. This tool has handles that stay cool, and the business end is rubber-dipped and curved to match the curvature of a jar. I have an old one and a newer model; the only difference is the newer one has plastic-covered handles and my older one has wooden handles. They both work equally well.

Wooden Chopsticks (or a similar tool): When canning, there will be times when you need a long, straight object like a chopstick or the long handle of a wooden spoon. Really, you can use almost any (nonmetal) object that can safely be poked into a jar to release trapped air bubbles and move food around as needed so it fits better. I like using chopsticks because they are cheap and effective. You can also use skewers, as long as they're wooden—you don't want to damage the glass jars. One other advantage or using chopsticks or skewers is you can use them in a pinch for other tasks, such as lifting bands out of hot water. You can also purchase a plastic tool called a bubble freer that is designed specifically for this task.

Lid Lifter: Not to be confused with a jar lifter, this little tool is a must have. Once again, it comes into play when you're handling hot items—the best way to do anything at this stage is to do it safely. Your lids will be sitting in steaming-hot water and keeping them hot while they are being placed on jars is important. A lid lifter has a small magnet on the end that lifts the lid easily, allowing for an easy transfer to the jar. Before I owned one, I had to use tongs and it was often difficult to get the lids out of the water without burning myself at least a little. Save yourself from the same experience and buy a lid lifter.

Lid Wrench: While the recipes in this book recommend hand-tightening lids before canning, there are times when lids are tough to remove after canning. If you sometimes struggle with the lids on jars, this tool will make your life easier.

Dish Towels: I can't imagine canning without a clean stack of dish towels for a variety of tasks. I use linen towels so there is no lint, but you can also use tightly woven cotton blends that have no nap. Just avoid fluffy towels that leave lint behind! Use your towels as a landing place for jars when removing them from the canner, for wiping jar rims before adding the lid, and for cleaning up spills as soon as they happen. I also use my dish towels at various other times, to protect my hands from steam, for wiping off spoon handles if needed, etc. I start my canning session with at least 6 on the counter and usually end up using every one. I recommend white towels that don't look like your everyday towels, so you keep them just for canning and bleach them as needed.

Knives: I was taught a sharp knife is safer than a dull one and I have yet to find any evidence to the contrary. Canning involves a lot of food prep, and that means a lot of cutting. Sharp knives reduce hand fatigue and help you cleanly cut uniform pieces of food. You will not need a large number of knives; a paring knife and an 8- or 10-inch (20 to 25.4 inch) chef's knife will suffice. Keep them super sharp and learn how to cut properly with each if you don't already have strong knife skills. A little time spent learning will immediately pay you back in saved prep time.

Measuring Cups: Plastic, metal, or glass, it doesn't matter which you choose as long as the markings are clear. What is important is having more than one set of measuring cups available. Having a second (or third) set at the ready will save you from stopping to clean in the middle of canning.

Measuring Spoons: Just as with measuring cups, it's essential to have a spare set of spoons if you don't want to be caught unprepared while canning. Also, as much as I love the novelty of newer measuring spoons that slide or adjust to the measurement you need, I don't think they're as reliable for exact measurements—especially when measuring liquids. I stick to the easy-to-read, standard measuring spoons that have served cooks well for generations.

Saucepans or Stockpots: Stainless steel or enamel-surfaced pots and pans work best when preparing recipes for canning. Aluminum and copper pans are considered "reactive" and will impart a metallic taste to acidic foods.

Rubber Spatulas: While not necessary for every recipe, they are perfect for scraping out and moving sticky items such as jams and jellies. Rubber spatulas are easy to clean and they don't absorb flavors. They are also safer to use inside glass jars. I buy the type with a rubber end that can be removed from the handle for better washing and sanitizing.

Tongs: You probably have a pair of tongs in your kitchen already. They're perfect for handling hot food while keeping your hands far away—and that's true whether you're grilling or canning. I prefer the longer style that most people use for the grill, but shorter tongs will work as well.

Pot Holders: Remember that even the thickest pot holder will allow steam through the fabric, so use them with caution. Having said that, pot holders are the tool of choice for moving hot, heavy pots around your stove. They can also insulate hot jars if you need to set one down on a cool countertop. Use a pot holder in a situation like this to avoid the possibility of cracking the glass jar or damaging your counter.

Ladles: A ladle should have a long handle and although I love metal for many utensils, for ladles, plastic rules! Why? A ladle will spend quite a bit of time in boiling-hot foods when canning and a metal handle can conduct heat. The last thing you want is a ladle that's too hot to handle! I most often use a plastic ladle rated for high temperatures that measures ½ cup (120 ml) of liquid and can double as a measuring device in a pinch.

Wooden Spoons: Wooden spoons will not become soft or excessively bendable when submerged in hot liquid, unlike some cheaper plastic spoons. I use wooden spoons when cooking, and canning is no different. Actually, it just gives you the opportunity to use a wooden spoon even more—for example, you can use the handle for releasing trapped air bubbles.

Nonessential (But Helpful) Equipment

These items are not necessary for canning most recipes. However, some will make your life easier for every recipe and others are essential for a smaller group of recipes—such as jams and jellies.

Food Processor: This is definitely not a "need it" item, but once you have one it is hard to go back. I use my food processor most often for shredding; it produces even results, and it greatly speeds up the job. I also use my food processor's slicing blade to cut thin slices for pickles. If you're on the fence about buying a food processor, borrow a friend's for a weekend. You will quickly see whether the speed and convenience are worth the cost (and cleanup).

Food Mill: A food mill is designed to purée fruits and vegetables. It removes the seeds and skins as well. It's the surefire way to get silky smooth applesauce and the smooth consistency you crave in some recipes. Food mills were once hard to find, but now are sold in most big box stores. You also may get lucky and find a used model in good shape. While I don't recommend buying a crucial piece of equipment second hand, such as an old pressure canner, a used food mill is a different story. If cleaned well after every use and used carefully, this useful tool will last for many years.

Jelly Bag: A jelly bag might sound like a very specialized tool, but it can be used for much more than just jelly. It is used to strain juice from fruits and vegetables after cooking. You transfer the produce to the bag and hang it over a pot or bowl so the juice can drip out and be collected.

Candy Thermometer: This is a cooking thermometer, inserted vertically into a mixture, with adjustable hooks or clips that allow it to be attached to the pot. It is useful when making jams and jelly to test for doneness when a specified temperature is reached.

Headspace Tool: This is a plastic tool designed to measure the headspace in the jar. It is often a combination bubble freer and headspace tool.

Timer: Yes, you can use the timer on your stove for canning. However, having a dedicated timer you can slip in your pocket is handy. Find a timer you can hear easily, and one that can get splashed without damage. (This probably means buying one with a midrange price point.) I set my timer as soon as my pressure canner reaches the correct pressure and slip it into my apron. If I get distracted (as much as I tell you not to, life does happen), I have a backup reminder that my jars are ready.

Labels: Labels are one item that may seem frivolous to beginners. After all, you can simply write the contents and date you preserved them on the metal lid. Yet, labels have their place. Good labels adhere to the glass jars, making it simple enough to identify the contents and date without handling the jars to peek at the tops. Labels are also more attractive and, thus, are a nice touch if you're making the recipes as gifts—or if your cupboard is in view from your kitchen or dining room.

I use labels on my jars and try to change them each year. This means at a glance I know the quantity that is left from a given year—helpful especially on a shelf that has many of the same things, like tomatoes. With unique year-based labels, I know quickly that there are four more quarts (946 ml) to be used up before we start eating this year's supply. So, labels are not critical to the canning process, but the more you can, the more you'll want to invest in at least simple labels.

COMMON CANNING TERMS

These terms are used throughout this book and the canning world. Once you understand the terminology, canning becomes a breeze.

Altitude: This is the elevation above sea level.

Blanch: This is the process of submerging food under boiling water for a few minutes, to loosen the skin or to stop enzymatic action in it. After blanching, the food is often placed in ice-cold water to stop the blanching process.

Boil: This is the process of heating liquid to 212°F (100°C), when bubbles break the surface.

Botulism: This is a form of food poisoning caused by ingesting the spores of Clostridium botulinum. The spores need an anaerobic environment (no oxygen) to survive. Botulism can be fatal.

Brine: This is a salt and water mixture used when pickling foods.

Canning Salt: This is salt that contains no iodine or noncaking agents. It is the salt used in most canning recipes.

Chutney: This is a thick recipe of sweet fruits and savory vegetables cooked with spices and vinegars.

Clear Jel: This is a modified food starch that will not break down when heated to a high temperature. It is a common thickener for canning foods.

Cold Pack (or Raw Pack): Raw food is placed in jars to be canned.

Headspace: This is the distance between the top of the food and the top of the mouth of the canning jar. Each canning recipe has a specified headspace.

High Acid: High acid refers to a food's pH of 4.6 or lower. High-acid foods include most fruits and pickled foods. Most of these foods do not need to be canned in a pressure canner.

Hot Pack: Hot pack is the method of heating food in hot liquid before placing it into jars.

Low Acid: These are foods with a pH higher than 4.6. Low-acid foods must be pressure canned.

Mason Jar: This is a glass jar designed for heating foods and liquids. Mason jars can withstand the high pressure of a canner and should not be substituted with other food jars.

Oxidation: This is the reaction that occurs when cut fruits and vegetables are exposed to the air, such as apples turning brown.

Processing: This is the length of time necessary for canned food to remain in the pressure cooker to be completely heated throughout.

Purée: This is the process of blending food to a smooth, even consistency.

Saucepan: This is a heavy pot with a broad flat bottom and deep sides. Saucepans come in many sizes.

Screw Band: This is a metal band with threads, used to attach the canning lid to the jar.

Simmer: This is the process of heating a liquid until numerous tiny bubbles rise to the surface.

Sterilize: This is a method used to kill all microorganisms.

Safety First

This section will demystify the canning process and put to rest notions that canning is hard, complicated, or dangerous.

The four simple steps to safe canning are:

1. Sterilize

Take a few minutes to complete these important steps at the beginning of any canning session.

Basic Steps:

- Boil water. Submerge all jars, lids, and any kitchen tools you will be using for 2 minutes in boiling water.
- Gather clean dish towels for the countertops and for wiping down the jars.
- Clean kitchen surfaces with hot water and a touch of vinegar.
- Make sure your hands are squeaky clean.

2. Select

Not all foods are canned the same way. Some use a boiling water bath canner and others require a pressure canner. It's important to know which canning method you will be using and to have the proper equipment.

Foods with a low pH (meaning they are more acidic) require the basic, boiling water bath method where the water reaches 212°F (100°C), or boiling temperature. Fruits, tomatoes with added acid, and pickles can be canned this way.

Higher pH foods (foods that are less acidic) require a pressure canner, which reaches 240°F (116°C).

Higher pH foods require the increased temperature to kill off all bacteria, so it's important to follow the selection guidelines carefully. Vegetables, meats, and any stocks or soups must be processed using a pressure canner. Refer to quick reference guides on pages 15-16.

3. Seal

Sealing occurs when a jar covered with a dome lid is processed in either a boiling water bath or a pressure canner. Ensuring you have a good, tight seal is critical to preserving your food.

Each lid has two parts—an outer ring and an inner panel with a rubber seal. Make sure both parts are sterilized and intact. The outer rings may be reused, but be sure to use new dome lids for every use.

A few tips to ensure a good seal:

Make sure to leave the recommended amount of headspace in your jar. Headspace is the amount of room left between the top of the food and lid. Too much room, and your food will spoil on top; too little room and a vacuum seal cannot be created. Strong acid foods need ¼ inch (6 mm) of headspace; low acid foods need ½ inch (1.3 cm) of headspace.

Once jars have processed and cooled, turn upside down to check for leaks. Make sure each one is sealed by pressing slightly on the center of the dome lid. If the lid makes a hollow popping sound and moves up and down, it isn't sealed. When this happens, refrigerate the jar and eat the contents within two weeks.

4. Store

Just two simple steps here:

First—Make sure to label your jars with the canning date and contents. Home-canned food will last up to twelve months.

Second—Store your canned jars in a cool, dark spot. Never store cans near a heat source, such as hot pipes, furnace vents or radiators, or a sunny window. This will harm the quality of your food.

I invert my canning jars for storage. This keeps the top layer of the food from drying out. Before storing jars, remove screw-top rings.

WHAT'S PH?

All cooking is chemistry—and in canning, it's the pH value of your food that matters most.

The simplest way to remember pH is that ***fruits, pickled foods*** and ***tomatoes with added vinegar or lemon juice*** (high-acid foods) use a ***boiling water bath canning method***. Everything else needs a ***pressure canner***, which reaches 240°F (116°C) to kill off all bacteria.

Why is this? It's because the dreaded botulism-causing bacteria don't survive in foods with a pH of 4.6 or less, so it's safe to process them in boiling water with a temperature of 212°F (100°C). Other foods require higher temperatures to be safely processed.

Quick Reference Guide to Selecting Canning Method

Chart 1: pH Value of Various Foods

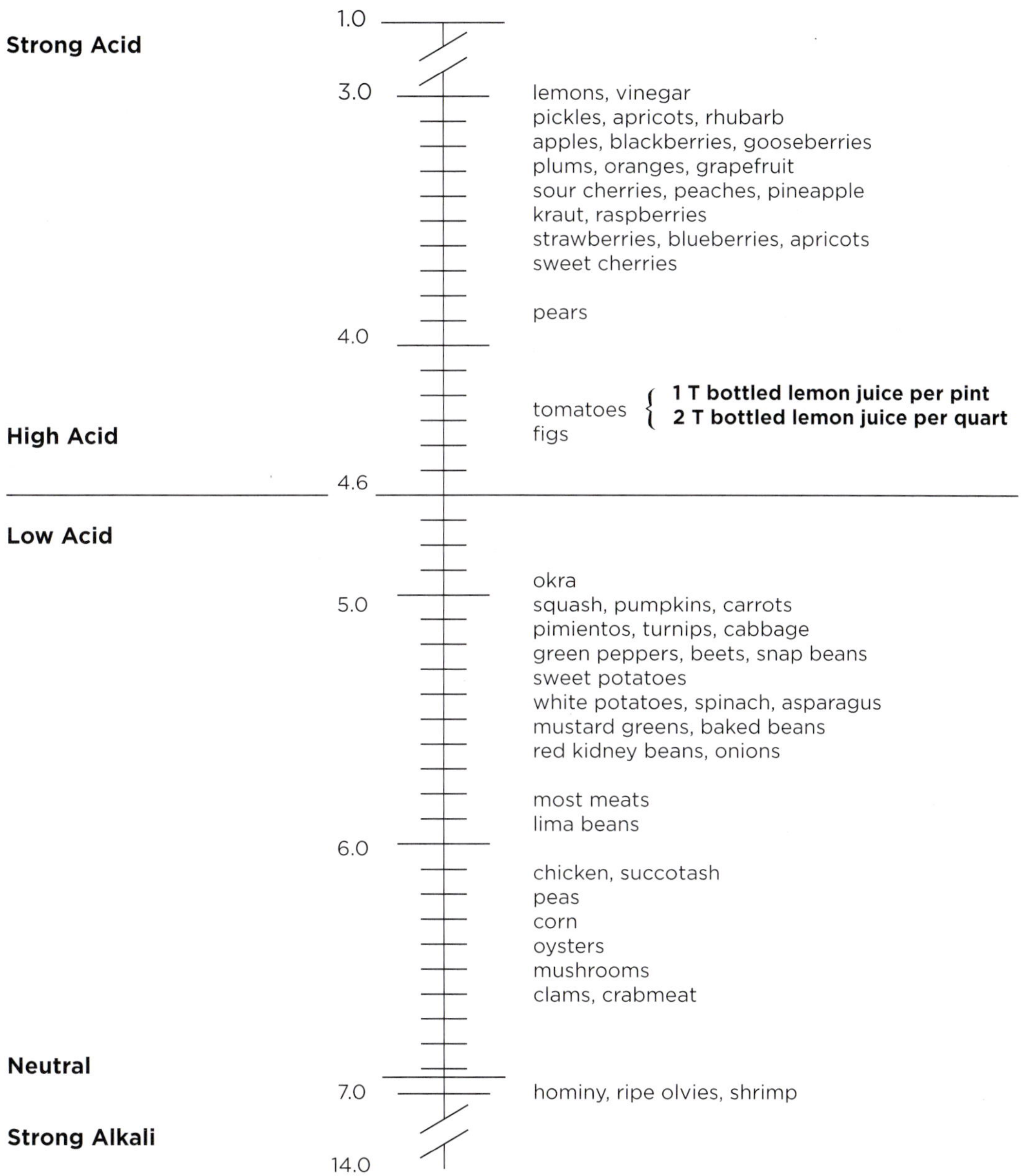

Yearbook of Agriculture, 1977

Chart 2: Temperatures for Food Preservation

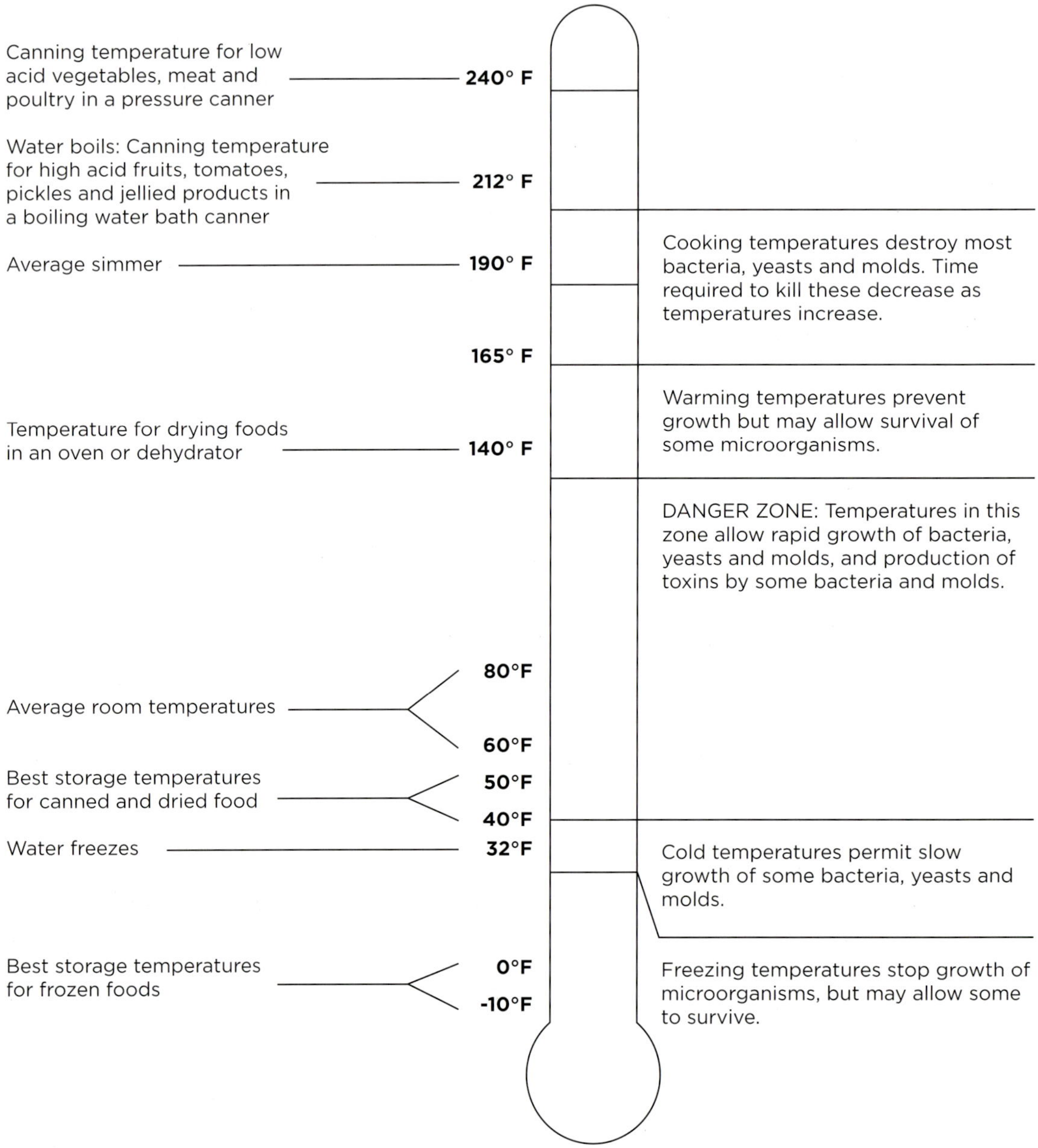

Determine Canning Method

High-acid foods like fruits, pickled foods, and tomatoes
Use a Boiling Water Bath

Low-acid foods such as vegetables, meats, and soups
Use a Pressure Canner
10 pounds (68.9 kPa) pressure kills botulism.
**Remember to heat all low-acid foods before eating.*

What Can I Can?

Here's a quick summary of what we've learned so far:

In a boiling water bath you can can:

- All fruits
- Tomatoes with extra acid (lemon juice or vinegar) added
- Pickles

In a pressure cooker you can can:

- Vegetables (beets, carrots, potatoes, squash cubes)
- Beans
- Meats
- Stocks and brothy soups

Do NOT can:

- Grains and starches (including rice and pasta, even if they're in soups)
- Oils
- Dairy products
- Puréed winter squash or pumpkin (see recipe on page 44 for a solution)
- Thickeners, such as cornstarch or flour

When you can, ALWAYS:

- Use fresh ingredients. Any blemishes on produce should be cut out.
- Follow all directions and recipes to the letter.
- Know your altitude and adjust processing instructions accordingly.
- Sterilize your jars, lids, and equipment before you begin.
- Keep a journal—it's great to have as a guide for next time.
- Have fun!

Planning for Canning

Canning is a method of food preservation that requires common sense. You can play around with ingredients, invent new recipes, and even make artistic labels that wow your friends, but *cleanliness* and *organization* are the keys to germ-free jars of food.

The most important rule for canning, and especially pressure canning, is **keep the process clean and simple**. This means keeping the work area and equipment as clean as you possibly can. You should also avoid nonstandard jars and any clutter—such as jar decorations—until after the food is ready for the pantry. You want as tidy a workspace as possible, especially as you're just getting started.

Following are other important things to consider when planning for canning:

- Start in the garden: grow what you like.
- Choose your ingredients wisely—freshest and ripest.
- Know the proper steps to canning.
- Prepare and pack the right way.
- Use reliable, tested recipes.
- Update your canning knowledge.

Let's look at each more closely.

Choose Your Ingredients Wisely

Always start with the freshest and ripest ingredients you can. This means you should be prepared to can before you shop. Even if you don't have the specific recipe ready to go, you can have all the equipment—jars, lids, rings, jar lifter, funnel, etc.—ready before you start. At a minimum, take inventory so if you're out of something, like jars or lids, you can pick them up when you go shopping.

It might be tempting to can less-than-perfect produce. Sure, canning "ugly" vegetables is okay. Sometimes you'll find tomatoes, carrots, or other vegetables that taste great but have an odd shape or other imperfection. These are fine for canning! However, *avoid canning wilted, soft, or bruised foods.* Starting with bruised or damaged food can give decay and bad bacteria that come with it a head start. Softer vegetables will also be even softer after canning, which most often works against your recipe. Use only firm, ripe foods at their peak of freshness.

Using fresh, local produce that your family loves is the best place to start with canning.

Know the Steps to Canning

Successful canning means getting food quickly from the market or garden into jars. We'll cover the basic steps on page 13 and you should be familiar with them and your recipe *before* you start your work. The middle of a recipe isn't the time to look something up. Even now, at the beginning of a season, I do a dry run through the process, pretending to can. It may look silly, but many times I realize I don't have a funnel or enough dish towels. My canning kitchen looks quite different from my regular kitchen; many items on my counters are put away and I have clear access around the room.

Prepare and Pack the Right Way

Even the most pristine fruits and vegetables require preparation for canning. For one, you'll want to wash off any dirt—or scrub, in the case of root vegetables. You'll also remove stems, leaves, and any part of the plant you don't want to eat (such as a tough end of a rhubarb stalk).

Beyond cleaning and cutting, you'll also be following a recipe to cold pack or hot pack your produce. Cold packing, also known as raw packing, is exactly what it sounds like: packing raw vegetables or fruit in the hot jars and pouring hot liquid over top before canning. Hot packing, on the other hand, will have you cooking your vegetables or fruit before adding them—and often the cooking liquid—to the jars. If this seems overwhelming, don't worry; your recipe will always be your guide on whether to cold or hot pack the jars.

Cutting uniformly sized pieces is key to ensuring the food in the jars cooks evenly.

Use Reliable, Tested Recipes

This can be a sensitive topic. Many cooks have emotional ties to recipes—and their historical significance—especially when it comes to something as classic as canning. The conflict comes from techniques or recipes that have since been proven unsafe. This is one area where caution rules. If you have an heirloom recipe, you can certainly find an updated version of it from a reliable source. You may also be able to troubleshoot the unsafe issue—say, by increasing the time of cooking to match modern standards. When all else fails, can the jars based on the most delicate ingredient. So, if you were to can your Great-Auntie M's famous chicken soup, use the most modern techniques for canning chicken soup you can find and can it in a pressure cooker under the correct pressure for that ingredient.

As much as I am a scratch cook who doesn't always stick to a recipe, when it comes to canning foods, following the rules is the only way. Changing things such as seasonings and how sweet you make a sugar syrup is fine, but be certain to follow canning recipes carefully and **do not experiment with time and temperature**.

Update Your Canning Knowledge

Each year, I review the USDA's online guidelines for safe canning techniques. While my grandmother certainly knew what she was doing, I do things a little differently, and the next generation of canners will, too. We continue to learn ways to improve techniques, safety, and recipes as the years go by. It's always a good idea to keep abreast of best practices. Recipes and techniques are often handed down through families, and it can be hard to change or give something up, but remember safety is key.

In this book, we'll be referencing the most current USDA guidelines at the time of writing in 2017. While there may be further updates or minor adjustments if a new style of pressure cooker is introduced, these guidelines will serve you well overall no matter the year.

Boiling Water Bath Canning

Before you begin, gather the necessary equipment. To can using the boiling water bath method, you will need a canner, canning rack, jars, lids, funnel, jar lifter, sauce or stock pans, and possibly a candy thermometer. See Canning Equipment on page 7 for details.

Follow these basic steps to make home canning simple and safe:

1. Follow the sterilization instructions on page 13.
2. Fill your boiling water bath canner two-thirds full with water and bring to a boil. You want enough water so that when you submerge the jars, the water level remains 2 inches (5 cm) above the lids. Adding vinegar (2 tablespoons [28 ml] or a good splash) helps if you have hard water. Minerals in hard water tend to form a cloudy surface on your jars. Vinegar helps keep the minerals in the water and off your jars.
3. Prepare your canning recipe, using only recipes meant for home canning. Fill your sterilized jars with the food, leaving the recommended amount of headspace. Use a nonreactive kitchen utensil, such as narrow rubber spatula or a bamboo skewer, to remove air bubbles. Air bubbles can cause uneven heating during processing and may impair the jar's ability to seal. Using a clean dish towel or paper towel, wipe the rims of the jars. This removes any spilled liquid or food, which can also prevent the jar from sealing. Place a dome lid on top of the jar and secure with a jar ring, screwing on so it's secure but not tight.
4. Submerge the jars into the canner with boiling water. Water should be 2 inches (5 cm) above the tops of the jars. ALWAYS place jars on a rack. If you don't have the rack made specifically for your canner, use a steamer basket or some other method to elevate the jars off the bottom of the canner. Jars that come into contact with direct heat through the bottom of the canning pot can crack and break.
5. Place the lid on the canning pot. Once the water returns to a boil, begin timing. Process for the number of minutes specified by the recipe, adjusting for altitude if necessary.
6. Once the processing time has elapsed, use the jar lifter to remove the jars from the boiling water. Place them on a dish towel on your countertop and let them rest until cooled. After 24 hours, test the seals by pressing slightly on the center of the dome lid. If the lid makes a hollow popping sound and moves up and down, it isn't sealed. When this happens, refrigerate the jar and eat the contents within 2 weeks. Make sure to label canned foods with the recipe name and date the item was canned. Store in a cool, dry place. Eat within a year.

ADJUST FOR ALTITUDE

Altitude matters for cooking in general and home canning in particular. Altitude affects the cooking temperature, so take a moment to look up your altitude (also called elevation) online and follow the canning instructions accordingly.

If you live in an area with an altitude above 1,000 feet (305 m), increase processing time by 2 minutes for every 1,000 (305 m) additional feet above sea level when using the boiling water bath method.

For pressure canning, you will need to increase the pressure settings for areas in higher altitudes.

MEASURING UP!

Because individual fruits of the same kind can vary so much in size, for the sake of accuracy, most of the recipes in this book call for fruit by weight. If you're planning to do a lot of jam making, a digital kitchen scale is an excellent investment. There are relatively inexpensive models available (around twenty dollars), and with a scale at your disposal, you'll know you're using the correct amount of fruit in your recipe. If you don't have a scale at home, weighing your fruit when you purchase it at the grocery store or farmers' market is another good option.

That said, there are times when weighing just isn't an option. If you're itching to make jam but don't have a scale handy, the following chart will help you determine how much fruit you'll need for different recipes in this book. Keep in mind the quantities are approximate, and may vary based on the size of the fruit.

FRUIT (FRESH)	WEIGHT	UNIT OR VOLUME EQUIVALENT
Apples	1 pound (455 g)	3 medium apples
Apricots	1 pound (455 g)	5 to 8 medium apricots
Blackberries	1 pound (455 g)	3½ cups (508 g) whole blackberries
Blueberries	1 pound (455 g)	4 cups (580 g) blueberries
Cherries (sweet)	1 pound (455 g)	3 cups (465 g) whole cherries
Figs	1 pound (455 g)	13 to 14 small to medium figs
Grapes (sweet)	1 pound (455 g)	3 cups (450 g) whole large grapes
Grapefruits	1 pound (455 g)	1 to 2 medium grapefruits
Kiwis	1 pound (455 g)	5 to 6 medium kiwis
Lemons	1 pound (455 g)	4 to 6 medium lemons
Limes	1 pound (455 g)	5 to 8 medium limes
Mangoes	1 pound (455 g)	2 small mangoes
Nectarines	1 pound (455 g)	3 medium nectarines
Oranges	1 pound (455 g)	2 to 3 medium oranges
Peaches	1 pound (455 g)	3 medium peaches
Pears	1 pound (455 g)	3 small to medium pears
Plums (sweet)	1 pound (455 g)	4 to 6 medium plums
Raspberries	1 pound (455 g)	2 (level) pints (473 ml each)
Rhubarb trimmed	1 pound (455 g)	4 to 8 stalks, or 3½ to 4 cups (427 to 488 g) medium dice
Strawberries	1 pound (455 g)	1 (level) quart (946 ml), whole

Can Your Jam

Once your jam is done, it's time to get it in the can—or rather, the jars. Don't worry if your jam looks a bit soupy at this point because this is normal; jam doesn't fully jell until after canning and after it's completely cool. Assuming you've followed all the previous steps, you're ready to can.

Filling Your Jars

It's important that both the jam and the jars are hot when filling the jars, so once you start canning, you'll want to move promptly so they don't cool off. Follow these steps and you'll have smooth sailing:

1. Take the lid off the canner. Use a jar lifter or tongs to remove one hot, sterilized jar at a time, dumping the water out of the jar and back into the canner as you go. Place hot, empty jars on a clean dish towel or cooling rack on the counter. There's no need to dry the jars—it's okay if they are wet. Once all the jars are removed, place the lid back on the canner and crank the heat up so that the water can return to a boil while you're filling your jars.
2. Using a ladle and canning funnel, ladle hot jam into each jar, being careful not to overfill the jars. If you need to pick up or move the jars, don't forget to use a large pot holder or dish cloth—these jars are hot!
3. Stick a bubble freer (or similar tool) down into the jam all the way to the bottom of the jar, hold the bubble freer flat against the inside edge of the jar, and then gently run it all the way around the inside edge of each jar to release any trapped air bubbles.
4. Using a headspace tool, measure the headspace of each jar. The headspace is the distance between the top of the jam and the top rim of the jar. To measure it, simply hold the headspace tool very gently on the surface of the jam, against the inside rim of the jar, and measure the distance from the surface of the jam to the very top of the jar. Most jam and jelly recipes call for ¼ inch (6 mm) of headspace, though always check your recipe. Using a small spoon, add or remove jam from each jar as necessary to achieve the proper headspace, remeasuring if needed. If you don't have enough jam to completely fill your last jar, simply refrigerate that jar after cooling and enjoy right away (rather than processing it). Alternatively, you may use a plastic ruler to measure the distance between the top of the food and the rim of the jar.
5. Carefully wipe the top rim of each jar with a clean, damp cloth or paper towel to remove any jam. This is where the lid meets the jar—ensuring that it's clean will help achieve a good seal.
6. Using a lid lifter, also called a magnetic lid wand, remove the lids one at a time from the simmering water in the small pot (the lids will be wet, but there's no need to dry them) and center a lid on the top of each jar. Gently place a screw band down over each lid and screw the band onto the jar until you meet resistance—and then tighten just a tiny bit more. This is known as fingertip tight. Do not overtighten the bands, as air needs to escape from the jar during processing.

Loading the Canner

Remove the lid from the canner and using a jar lifter, gently lower each jar down into the boiling water and place it on the rack in the canner. (If the boiling water is making it hard to see, you can turn the heat down temporarily as you're placing the jars.) Ideally, you'll want to hold the jars by their bodies, not by their necks, so that you don't dislodge the lids and the screw bands. Be careful not to let the jars tip over—and if they do, right them immediately. Also, make sure the jars are not touching each other or the sides of the canner and that there is at least 1 to 2 inches (2.5 to 5 cm) of water covering all of the jars. This allows water to circulate freely and thoroughly around all parts of every jar during processing, which will ensure that the jam is subject to the temperature necessary to kill any microorganisms. If, after you've placed your jars in the canner, you find that they are not covered sufficiently with water, add more hot water to the canner as needed.

Processing Your Jars in the Canner

After you've loaded the canner, place the lid on it, crank the heat up to high, and bring the water to a rolling boil. Once the water is at a rolling boil, you can start your processing time. Set your timer for the specific processing time indicated in your recipe—usually 10 minutes for jams and jellies, but always double-check. If you're at 1,000 feet (304.8 m) or more of elevation, you'll need to increase your processing time (see "Adjust for Altitude!" on page 20 for more information). After the processing is complete, turn off the heat and allow the canner and jars to sit—untouched—for 5 minutes. This 5-minute waiting period is important. If you remove your jars from the canner immediately, jam will sometimes seep out of them—an occurrence known as siphoning—due to the dramatic change in temperature and pressure. The 5-minute waiting period allows the jam to cool down enough before coming out of the canner that siphoning is unlikely to occur. Be sure that you don't wait longer than 5 minutes, however, as exposure to heat for too long a period may cause your jam not to jell properly.

WHAT'S ALL THAT RACKET IN THERE?

During processing, there's a lot going on in your canning pot. Boiling water circulates around the jars, heating them to the required temperature (212°F [100°C] at sea level for boiling water bath canning) and exposing the food in the jars to that temperature for the specified processing time. As the food heats up it expands, forcing air out of the jars. After processing, when the jars begin to cool, the food shrinks, and because the air was forced out of the jars during processing, when the food shrinks, the lids get sucked down. This creates a vacuum seal, which will keep out contaminants and allow the sealed jar of food to be safely stored at room temperature.

Removing Your Jars from the Canner

After the canner has cooled for 5 minutes, it's time to remove the jars. Using a jar lifter, carefully lift the jars from the canner one at a time, always keeping them upright, and place them on a dish towel or cooling rack on the counter, with space in between each jar. There will likely be a small pool of water on the top of each jar when you take it out, but don't worry about that—the water will evaporate as the jar cools. It's tempting to check out your jam, move the jars around, and handle the jars in general, but refrain! This cooling period is when your jars are in the process of sealing, and the less you handle your jars during this time, the more likely you are to get a proper seal. Allow your jars to cool, untouched, for 12 to 24 hours. You sometimes (though not always) will hear little popping noises as the jars cool—don't worry. This popping is a good thing! It's the little "button" on the top of the lid sucking down, and it's usually a good indication that a jar is in the process of sealing.

Checking Your Seals and Storing Your Jars

After your jars have cooled for at least 12 hours, you'll want to check them to ensure that each jar has sealed properly. To do this, press gently with your finger into the center of each lid. If the "button" that is in the center of each lid is already depressed, and there is no movement when you press down, then you have a proper vacuum seal. If the "button" is not depressed, and there is movement when you press on it, then your jar did not seal properly.

If a jar doesn't seal (which occasionally does happen), you have a couple of options. You may want to re-can your jam, though this is the most labor-intensive option. To do this, you'll need to dump out the jar, reheat the jam to boiling, and reprocess it in a clean, hot jar with a new lid for the recommended amount of time. I tend to go for an easier option—if I'm planning on eating it right away, I'll put it in the refrigerator. It will keep this way for about 3 weeks. Or, if I'm looking for longer-term storage, I'll freeze the jam, as it will keep in the freezer for about 6 months. Freezing it right in the jar is just fine, though make sure the jam is cool first and be sure to remove the lid and take out a couple of spoonfuls so that there is at least ½ inch (1.3 cm) of headspace before re-capping and freezing. This will allow room for the jam to expand when it freezes.

Fortunately, jars do seal properly most of the time. After you've confirmed that your jars have sealed, remove the screw bands. (You'll notice that the bands are already quite loose—this is normal!) It may seem counter-intuitive to take the bands off, but at this point, each lid is adhering to the jar because of the vacuum seal; the screw bands are no longer doing anything useful and can cause various problems during storage if left on. After removing the screw bands, wash them, thoroughly dry them, and then store them for future use. (It's helpful to keep bands nearby, so you can easily reach for one to put on after opening a jar or when giving a jar as a gift!) Then, rinse the outside of your sealed jars thoroughly to remove any jam that may have gotten on the outside of the jar during filling or processing. Dry your jars, clearly label and date them, and store them—preferably in a clean, dry, dark location between 50 and 70°F (10 to 21°C). Your sealed jars of jam will keep well this way for up to one year.

Before you open up a jar that has been stored, it's always a good idea to make sure the jar is still vacuum sealed. To do this, check that the button in the center is still depressed, and with your fingers, very gently try to pull up the lid, making sure that it doesn't budge. You'll also want to visually inspect the jam. If you notice any obvious signs of spoilage, discard immediately. If your jar was processed correctly, it should be fine, but seal failures and spoilage occasionally do occur during storage, so it's always important to check.

You may notice when you're examining your jar that the jam has separated, but don't be alarmed—this is normal for many jams and is not a sign of spoilage. When you open a jar of jam that has separated, simply mix it up well. Opening up a properly vacuum-sealed jar typically requires more than hands alone—I use a butter knife or other metal kitchen utensil to carefully pry lids off. After you open one of your jars of jam, store it in the refrigerator, capped with a lid and a screw band. It will keep this way for about three weeks.

Pressure Canning Basics

Have you ever wondered why pressure canning works? It's actually a simple concept, and, if you are a bit of a science geek like me, quite fascinating!

The goal of pressure canning is to expose food to a high temperature under a specific pressure for a specific period of time to destroy microorganisms that are harmful if eaten. Pressure canning allows food to be heated to 240°F (116°C)—the temperature necessary to destroy these microorganisms, including the botulism bacteria.

Botulism is rightfully one of the biggest fears for those new to canning or those who don't can. It is flavorless and odorless. Even worse, it cannot be destroyed by boiling or hot water bath canning, which only reaches 212°F (100°C) regardless of how long you boil the food. Botulism thrives in low-acid foods, in moist environments, and in an anaerobic (no oxygen) environment. All these conditions are present inside an *improperly* processed jar of food. Luckily, proper pressure canning creates a higher-temperature environment and can eliminate the risk of botulism in hours.

The other big fear when it comes to pressure canning is the safety of the pressure canner itself. Through the rest of this section, we'll discuss pressure canners, essential equipment, and using the pressure canner for the first time. By the end of this section, your fear should be a thing of the past, replaced by excitement to try your first recipe!

Pressure Canning Equipment

When I started canning, I was a purist. I wanted to pretend my grandmother was a homesteader and she was teaching me her ways in the kitchen. I wanted to use only equipment she would have used—and everything needed to have a history. Soon, though, the reality was I needed to can large quantities to feed my growing family. There just weren't enough hours in the day to hand-shred 50 pounds (22.7 kg) of zucchini!

As I started using my food processor, a professional-quality chef's knife, and recipes with precise measurements and clear instructions, my canning became more efficient—and productive. I still have some of my old-fashioned equipment, but it has found a new home—lovingly displayed on the top of my cupboards!

That said, the equipment needed for canning is not extensive and it is affordable. If you're an avid home cook, you may already own much of what you need except, perhaps, the canner itself. See Canning Equipment on page 7. Other than the canner, jars, and lids, most items are recommended for your convenience.

The Pressure Canner

A pressure canner is, essentially, a heavy kettle designed to withstand higher pressure than a normal pot. While models vary in their features, all pressure canners offer a few common elements.

Before we get into the nuts and bolts (for some models, I mean that literally!), know this:

as mentioned previously, a pressure cooker is not the same as a pressure canner. Yes, both devices use pressure and they look similar. However, pressure cookers are not designed for canning. Most models aren't large enough for cans and they don't have pressure gauges.

Pressure canners come in a wide range of models and sizes. When choosing the right model for you, consider how much you'll be canning at one time; for most people, a pressure canner in the 16- to 22-quart (15 to 21 L) range will do the trick. The other main differences will be the gauge type (dial versus weighted) and cover type (metal-to-metal or lock-on with gasket). Let's get to it.

Locking cover: All pressure canners have a locking cover that can be closed in only one correct position. There are canners with covers that lock on with a rubber gasket between the cover and kettle, and other canners that have individual locking wing nuts around the edge. I have both styles and still use them both every year. Neither one is better, objectively, but I find I reach for the model with the gasket and lock-on cover more often.

I do this because the locking process for the pots is different and I prefer the locking procedure on the cover with the gasket. Unlike a metal-to-metal cover, which requires manual tightening, lock-on covers with gaskets have a specific closing procedure with matching markings for the lid and pot and/or clamps. This means there's either a "locked" or "not locked" situation and no guessing as to the tightness of wing nuts. (Is this tight enough? Did I overtighten?)

NOTE

Weighted gauge models do not self-correct for altitude adjustments. This means at altitudes above sea level (higher than 1,000 feet [304.8 m]), the pressure you set should be adjusted upward. See the guidelines on page 32.

No matter which lid type you have, always follow the manufacturer's instructions for locking the lid. Also, note that if your lid has a gasket, you'll need to clean it according to your manufacturer's instructions and use care. For example, some models may tell you to lubricate gaskets with cooking oil while others do not. Any damage to a gasket can affect the machine's ability to hold pressure correctly. Regularly inspect your gasket and replace at the first sign of wear.

Pressure gauge: Another feature that all pressure canners share is a gauge that displays the pressure inside the canner. There are two types of gauges and both work equally well. The first type of gauge is a weighted gauge. This gauge has no dial face, but instead has numbers engraved around its edges. This gauge will rattle when the correct pressure is reached; then, it will rattle faster and allow some steam to escape if the pressure gets higher than necessary. Note that it's not better to have slow or fast jiggling with this type of pressure gauge. The fact that it is moving means it is maintaining the recommended pressure. In my opinion, this gauge is more foolproof as it requires less heat adjustment than a dial gauge.

The second type, a dial gauge, is an easy-to-read, clock face–style gauge. It has a hand that moves as the pressure increases. You adjust the heat while you watch the gauge. Start the timer once the canner gauge reaches the correct pressure and adjust the heat level with the goal of keeping the pressure gauge at the correct number for the period of time specified in the recipe.

As mentioned elsewhere, it's important to check your gauge for accuracy at least annually. The start of a new canning season is a great time to do this.

Your county's cooperative extension office should be able to help and some manufacturers offer this service as well.

Release valve and overpressure plug: On the cover of your pressure canner, there is a release valve, which can also be referred to as a vent tube, petcock, or pipe vent in the manufacturer's manual. This release valve needs to be checked at the start of each canning session. Simply hold the cover up and make sure you can see light through the vent tube. If not, clean it with a pipe cleaner or however the manufacturer recommends. Note that this valve is where steam will come out and there are models where the weighted gauge will be on the valve.

Your pressure canner will also have an overpressure plug or safety fuse. This is a simple release that functions as a backup to the primary release valve/vent tube. The overpressure plug opens if the pressure gets too high due to the release valve being blocked. It is a safety feature not present on old-style pressure canners, and you should not use a pot that's so old it does not have this important feature. This backup release mechanism is there for your safety. You should also look for the Underwriter's Laboratory (UL) seal to ensure the device's safety.

The manufacturer of your pot may have recommendations for keeping the release valve and overpressure plug clean and operational. Always follow the best practice directions for your pot.

Canning rack: Finally, your pressure canner will come with a rack. The rack will look like a circular dish with holes in it and it's designed to sit on the bottom of the canner. Jars will sit on top of the rack; its design allows for the circulation of steam around the jars. It also helps stabilize your jars so they don't knock together or against the sides of the canner (possibly breaking them). If your canner did not come with a rack or your rack breaks, you need to buy a new one. The best place to start is the canner's manufacturer. *Don't can without a rack.*

Let's Talk about Jars

Jars are about to become your new best friend. There are as many styles, sizes, shapes, colors, and uses for these sturdy glass containers as there are foods to put in them. Yet despite the fact that most jars have the same purpose (food preservation), not all jars are created equal.

The canning jars I recommend are the modern-style canning jars made by Ball and similar manufacturers. They are distinguished by their sturdy glass, clearly marked volumes, and 2-piece lids.

The main alternative to this style of jar is experiencing a resurgence, though more as a dry storage jar than for canning. This alternate style of jar, called a bail-type jar, made famous by Weck, has two glass pieces—the jar and the lid—that are sealed together using a rubber gasket. Metal clips or a wire were used in conjunction to hold the lid on while canning, but the rubber seal acts like the modern seal under the lid to create the airtight environment you need to can.

While this type of jar may be used for canning, I tend to recommend it for refrigerated or dry storage instead. Weck jars with brand-new rubber seals may be used if you follow the manufacturer's instructions, but they tend to fail the beginning canner more often. Even worse, similar-looking vintage jars may not be intended for pressure canning at all. If you collect glass jars to reuse for food storage like I do, keep them in rotation only for dry goods.

So, what other options do you have within the recommended type of jars? You have a variety of sizes to choose from. Most of the recipes in this book all come with a recommended jar size. Other considerations include the size of your canner, which may not accommodate the largest jars.

The other important consideration is the size of the jar's mouth opening. Canning jars commonly come with two options:

1. **Regular-mouth jars** have a small opening, about 2⅜ inches (6 cm), but are good for liquids such as stocks or juices, and brothy soups. While many canners use only regular-mouth jars and have no trouble, keep in mind that regular-mouth jars are a little harder to clean if there is residue inside.
2. **Wide-mouth jars** are my personal favorite for a few reasons. You can easily get a utensil inside to scrape them clean. I also like wide-mouth jars because, with their opening at about 3 inches (7.5 cm), the jars are easier to fill for recipes with larger pieces. If your recipe will retain a firm texture, it's easier to remove the vegetables when serving as well.

There are many canning jar sizes, from half pints (235 ml) all the way up to gallons (liters), although these large jars are not usually used by home canners. With even grocery stores selling canning jars these days, you can easily find the right jar for the job. Most of the recipes in this book, and elsewhere, recommend a specific size. For safety reasons, use the recommended size and don't switch up sizes unless there is a corresponding recommendation for canning. Let's look at some of the jars you'll use!

- **Jelly jar:** Not just for jellies and jams, these jars come in a range of sizes from 4 ounces (120 ml) to 12 ounces (355 ml). They are the perfect size for gifting and for the little condiments you want on the table, without having to eat from the container for an extended period of time. Can you imagine a quart (946 ml) of mustard, for example? Use jelly jars for mustards, ketchups, barbecue sauce, and small-batch recipes.

  Jelly jars can also highlight a particular food. Jelly jars have wide openings so you can get out every last bite, and they are easy to clean. Due to their size, they require less processing time, which can be an advantage come canning day.
- **Half pint:** The half-pint jar gets quite a bit of mileage in my kitchen. When it comes to volume, these jars hold 8 ounces (235 ml) of food—and they also have the benefit of a wide mouth. I think it's the perfect size jar for relishes, pickles, and chunky chutneys. I use them exclusively for foods I want to use up quickly.
- **Pint:** Pint jars hold 16 ounces (473 ml) and can be used for many items. I use pints for soups I want to package as single lunches, salsas, and specialty recipes like cocktail onions. Pints are a manageable size for most recipes unless you are canning for a large family.
- **Quart:** Speaking of canning for the whole family, quart jars are my biggest workhorse. Quarts hold 2 pints (946 ml), so you can package double the soup, sauce, etc. I always use quarts to can tomatoes, family-size recipes of sides like baked beans, and soups and broths meant to serve more at once. If you are canning sweet fruits, you may want to consider quart jars. It all depends on how fast your family goes through the food—in my house, the sweets go fast!

Caring for Your Canning Gear

Your pressure canner is a sturdy piece of equipment with simple parts. It does require some care, however. Before the canning season, inspect your canner and all the parts for any nicks or cracks. Check the cover and make sure the overpressure plug moves freely and the vent tube is unblocked. If your pressure canner has a rubber gasket, make sure it is pliable and clean.

Every year, the dial gauge on your pressure canner should be checked for accuracy. This is usually a free or inexpensive service that can be done at your local county extension office or hardware store. Do this early, as many services require that you drop off your equipment. If you wait until the last minute, you may have to wait for the return and miss a week or two of prime produce.

Between canning sessions, a quick rinse and dry of the pot is all that is needed before storage as long as you keep it clean as a matter of course. I keep my canner in the original box once it is clean and dry. That helps keep it from gathering dust and ensures it doesn't get dinged up. It also protects the gauge from damage.

When it comes to your canning jars, they are sturdy but, at the end of the day, they are glass. Run your hand gently over the rim of each jar the day before you want to use it to find any small nicks. Also, hold each jar up to the light and look at the glass. You will be able to see small cracks if there are any. Chips, nicks, and cracks are all signs the glass is no longer fit for canning. It is for this reason I never recommend letting your family use canning jars as drinking glasses. Something that seems as harmless as the teaspoon you stir your sweet tea with can weaken the glass. If you love the look of canning jars, buy a set just for drinking and keep the ones you use for canning stored separately.

The screw bands are the backbone of a good seal. When you purchase a box of canning jars, they come with the lid and band on each jar. The lids are not reusable, but the bands are. Once your jars cool, carefully remove the screw band and store the sealed jar. Screw bands can be reused until they become bent or corroded. Wash and dry your bands before storing them and plan to replace a few each year. I recommend keeping a box on hand for this purpose.

Likewise, keep measuring cups and spoons in good shape by keeping them clean. I like to keep all my canning supplies in the same drawer, and I like to sanitize my supplies before each canning session (see sidebar Clean is Best on page 33). This ensures my surfaces and items are as clean as possible before I start. Using plastic items means they can be sanitized without the risk of corrosion.

Every canning season should start with a visual inspection. This includes removing the lid and checking the gasket for some models.

The Pressure Canning Process

No matter what food you are preserving, it requires the same steps to pressure can.

- If you're using an electric pressure canner, you will need to rely on additional instructions from the manufacturer to achieve the desired pressure for the appropriate length of time—you will not adjust it with a stovetop burner like the other models.
- Likewise, if you're using a weighted-gauge model, consult the manufacturer's instructions on setting the canning pressure and for information on how to evaluate whether the canner is maintaining pressure.

The USDA specifically calls out a serious error that can cause unsafe canning:

As mentioned previously, the **internal canning temperature drops at high altitudes**. To correct for this, adjust the pressure of your canner upward if you live above sea level. USDA guidelines recommend increases as follows for **dial gauge canners**. The recipes in this book specify dial gauge pressure for canners below 2,000 feet (610 m).

For recipes at 11 pounds (75.8 kPa):

2,001 to 3,000 feet (610 m to 914.4 m) ....11½ pounds (79.3 kPa)

3,001 to 4,000 feet (914.7 m to 1.2 km) ....12 pounds (82.7 kPa)

4,001 to 5,000 feet (1.2 km to 1.5 km) ....12½ pounds (86.2 kPa)

5,001 to 6,000 feet (1.5 km to 1.8 km) ....13 pounds (89.6 kPa)

6,001 to 7,000 feet (1.8 km to 2.1 km) ....13½ pounds (93.1 kPa)

7,001 to 8,000 feet (2.1 km to 2.4 km) ....14 pounds (96.5 kPa)

8,001 to 9,000 feet (2.4 km to 2.7 km) ....14½ pounds (100 kPa)

9,001 to 10,000 feet (2.7 km to 3 km) ....15 pounds (103.4 kPa)

For recipes at 6 pounds (14.4 kPa):

2,001 to 4,000 feet (610 m to 1.2 km) ....7 pounds (48.3 kPa)

4,001 to 6,000 feet (1.2 km to 1.8 km) ....8 pounds (55.2 kPa)

6,001 to 8,000 feet (1.8 km to 2.4 km) ....9 pounds (62.1 kPa)

8,001 to 10,000 feet (2.4 km to 3 km) ....10 pounds (68.9 kPa)

CLEAN IS BEST

We all have clutter in our kitchens. As much as things make our house our home, they also collect dust and dirt.

When you are canning, clear your kitchen counters completely of anything you aren't using for the canning process. I remove all my small appliances, jars of utensils, and my extra measuring cups and storage containers. If I am not going to touch the item for canning, it gets removed.

This may seem like extra work, but it ensures the work area can be cleaned thoroughly. It also means you won't accidentally knock into something and ruin some of your hard work. If you're wondering where to put everything, do what I do: Make your kitchen table a temporary countertop! Sure, it clutters up the kitchen table, but that's okay. You won't be using it while you can.

CLEANING

Okay, is your counter free of all clutter? Great! Now it's time to wipe down all the surfaces with hot, soapy water to remove any grease and dirt. This is the cleaning step; it will remove any small particles of food or other impurities from your countertop. Only once your counter and work surfaces are clean are you ready to move on to sanitizing.

SANITIZING

To sanitize, you can use a commercial product, such as Star San. However, most people prefer to use what they have on hand: bleach. Create a sanitizing mixture by mixing 1 tablespoon (15 ml) of food-safe bleach with 1 gallon (3.8 L) of water. This concentration of bleach in water, 200 ppm, doesn't need to be rinsed off but it does need to air-dry before the surface is considered sanitized. Do what I do and pour the mixture in a spray bottle. Once you've cleaned your counter, mist it with the sanitizing solution and wipe so you have a thin layer across the surface. Let it air-dry and you're ready to move on to canning!

For **weighted gauge canners**, as soon as you get over 1,000 feet (304.8 m) in elevation, you should switch from the 5-pound (34.5 kPa) to the 10-pound (68.9 kPa) or the 10-pound (68.9 kPa) to the 15-pound (103.4 kPa) setting for safety, depending on the recipe. The recipes in this book specify pressure for weighted gauge canners below 1,000 feet (304.8 m).

If **air is trapped in your canner**, it lowers the temperature obtained at any pressure. Take care to avoid this.

Here is a quick review of the steps we'll take:

1. Prepare the canning area.
2. Prepare the canning jars and utensils.
3. Prepare the canner.
4. Prepare the food.
5. Fill the jars to the correct level.
6. Fill the canner.
7. Follow the recipe instructions.
8. Cool the jars.
9. Check the seals; label and store the jars.

Prepare the Canning Area

If you skipped the last page (go back and read it!), preparing the area means removing whatever you don't need to pressure can from the counter: extra utensils, small appliances, daily dishes, and other items should be placed elsewhere while you focus on canning. Clean and sanitize your countertops and anything else you think will come in contact with the canning jars and lids before they go into the canner.

Prepare the Canning Jars and Utensils

The jars and utensils you will use should be examined beforehand to make sure nothing is chipped or broken. The jars and utensils you will use should be washed in hot, soapy water before use. The clean jars should then be placed in hot—not boiling—water. Single-use lids need to be clean. It is no longer necessary to heat Ball or Kerr brand lids, but if you choose to heat them, do not boil them.

One tip for being ready to can is to place your jars in the dishwasher and run it through a sanitizing cycle. You can leave your jars in the dishwasher until you actually need to use them. I often do this the night before so they are waiting for me first thing in the morning. Before I had a dishwasher, I would wash them the night before and place them on linen hand towels on the sideboard. In the morning, all I had to do was place them in hot water to heat while I prepped my food.

Prepare the Canner

Follow the manufacturer's guidelines for filling your specific canner. You'll likely need to insert the canning rack, add 2 to 3 inches (5 to 7.5 cm) of water to the bottom of the canner, and get that water preheated.

Prepare the Food

Your recipe may require a variety of preparation techniques before you can it. Fruits or vegetables must be washed, and perhaps peeled, and cut according to the recipe guidelines. Some foods are also browned or otherwise precooked. When making broth or soup, you may cook the entire recipe before you can. In any case, your recipe will clearly provide these directions.

Fill the Jars to the Correct Level

Once your food is ready to can, the sanitized jars must be filled to the recipe's specifications. Nearly all recipes in this book provide cooking liquid or heated water to top up your jars to the proper fill level. Note that all recipes require some amount of headspace, the room between the top of the food or liquid and the rim of the jar. (Proper headspace allows the food to expand and air to be forced out during the canning process.) Once the jars are full, use a nonmetallic tool to remove any air bubbles. Wipe the rims with a clean damp cloth, carefully place the lids on, and hand-tighten the screw bands around the lids.

Fill the Canner

Gently place your jars in the canner on top of the canning rack, making sure they do not touch (using a jar lifter, grab the jars below the screw band). When the canner is full, double check that all jars are upright and not tilted. Place the lid on the canner and lock it according to the manufacturer's instructions.

If you accidentally prepared more food than will fit in your pressure canner, do not pack jars for the next batch and let them sit. Instead, I recommend repeating the steps here in the same order: prepare the food, prepare the canner, pack the jars, and then fill the canner once again.

Follow your manufacturer's guidelines to close and lock the pressure canner. If you're using a model with more manual controls, you typically need to secure the lid, open the petcock (vent pipe) or leave the weight off the vent port, and place the pot over high heat until steam flows continuously for about 10 minutes. At this point, it is time to close the petcock or vent port and let the canner pressurize—it should take less than 5 minutes. Again, always follow your machine's instructions as you must close and lock the lid properly to maintain pressure!

Follow the Recipe

With your lid locked in place, use your canner's settings or a stovetop burner to get a steady stream of steam from your pressure canner for 10 minutes or according to the manufacturer's guidelines. *Only once you do this should you close the vent and start bringing the canner to the proper pressure.*

For an electric pressure canner or a weighted-gauge model, you will most likely be instructed to set the pressure now. If you're using the stovetop to supply the heat, keep the pot at a temperature that maintains the pressure at or above the recommended level for the duration of the recipe's recommended processing time.

No matter which type of pressure canner you use, *start timing your recipe once the pressure on the dial gauge is correct or when the weighted gauge moves* as described by the manufacturer. In other words, if your recipe says the pressure should be held at 11 pounds (75.8 kPa) for 30 minutes, start the timer only once the pot reaches 11 pounds (75.8 kPa), not when you first apply the heat.

Pressure Dip?

Did your pressure dip below the recipe's recommended pressure? *The only safe way to remedy this is to bring the pot back to the recommended pressure and restart the timer.* **Never** let the timer continue once a pot falls below the recommended pressure amount as you can no longer guarantee the safety of the canned food.

Use care not to create large drops or increases in pressure, even above the recommended range, as this could prevent some of the jars from sealing properly. (Again, if you're using a weighted gauge, the manufacturer will provide instructions on how to monitor the pressure.)

Cool the Jars

Once your recipe is finished cooking, turn off the heat. After some of the cooling time has passed, you can safely remove the lid. The amount of time it takes before you can safely release pressure and remove the lid varies by machine. It's often about 10 minutes after the machine reaches 0 pounds (0.7 kPa) pressure.

Do not attempt to speed the cooling by putting your canner in the fridge or freezer or by placing it in a sink full of cold water. The canner needs to cool without your assistance. Trying to cool the canner faster can result in unsafe canned foods, as well as imperfect seals.

Once the lid is off, do not remove the jars immediately; let them continue to cool inside the canner for about 20 minutes. This is a good time to set up a place for the jars to rest once you remove them. I recommend setting a clean dish towel in an out-of-the way place in the kitchen, away from people who may be tempted to touch the cooling canned food and away from any drafts. You may need a spot for the cans to rest for up to 24 hours as they cool, so choose wisely!

Once you're ready to remove the jars, use a jar lifter to remove them and place them on the clean dish towel, about 1 inch (5 cm) apart. Do not disturb the jars while they cool and do not try to remove the bands yet. You will hear the jars "ping" as each lid finishes sealing during the cooling process.

Check the Seals and Label and Store the Jars

Once the jars cool to room temperature, remove the screw bands and check that each jar is sealed properly: Press gently on the lid. It should be concave (dip inward) if you have a good seal. It should feel firm to the touch and it should not move or dip when you push on it. Do not tip or shake the jars, but do wipe off any residue that may have escaped during the time in the canner. Label your jars and place the sealed jars in a cool, dry location. If you have any jars that did not seal properly, refrigerate them and use them within a week or two (depending on the recipe).

Chapter 2

Vegetables

Home canning is a great way to enjoy summer vegetables and make quick meals. My favorite veggies to can are beets, beans, and succotash made from corn and lima beans. I also can a lot of cubed winter squash, which makes great soups and squash risotto! There are a number of vegetables that are not recommended for home canning. Broccoli and cauliflower become discolored and their strong flavors are unpleasantly intensified. Summer squash, zucchini, cabbage, and eggplant become mushy and off-flavored as well.

Asparagus

METHOD: PRESSURE CANNING

PROCESSING TIME:
PINTS (473 ML) 30 MINUTES;
QUARTS (946 ML) 40 MINUTES

YIELD: 7 QUARTS (6.6 L)

24 pounds (10.9 kg) asparagus spears

1 teaspoon salt per jar (optional)

Wash and trim asparagus so spears can stand up in your jars.

Pack into hot, sterilized jars. Add a teaspoon of salt (optional). Fill jars with boiling water, making sure asparagus is fully submerged. Leave a 1-inch (2.5 cm) headspace.

Remove any air bubbles. Wipe rims and secure lids.

Process pints (473 ml) for 30 minutes and quarts (946 ml) for 40 minutes in pressure canner at pressure listed for your altitude and canner (see Adjust for Altitude! on page 20).

Beans, Green and Wax

METHOD: PRESSURE CANNING

PROCESSING TIME: 25 MINUTES

YIELD: 7 QUARTS (6.6 L)

14 pounds (6.4 kg) green or wax beans

1 teaspoon salt per jar (optional)

Wash and trim ends of beans. Snap into smaller pieces if desired.

Pack into hot, sterilized jars. Add a teaspoon of salt (optional). Fill jars with boiling water, covering beans. Leave a 1-inch (2.5 cm) headspace.

Remove any air bubbles. Wipe rims and secure lids.

Process pints (473 ml) and quarts (946 ml) for 25 minutes in pressure canner at pressure listed for your altitude and canner (see Adjust for Altitude! on page 20).

Carrots

METHOD: PRESSURE CANNING

PROCESSING TIME:
PINTS (473 ML) 25 MINUTES;
QUARTS (946 ML) 30 MINUTES

YIELD: 7 QUARTS (6.6 L)

20 pounds (9.1 kg) carrots, tops removed

1 teaspoon salt per jar (optional)

Wash, peel, and slice carrots to desired size.

Pack into hot, sterilized jars. Add a teaspoon of salt (optional). Fill jars with boiling water, covering carrots. Leave a 1-inch (2.5 cm) headspace.

Remove any air bubbles. Wipe rims and secure lids.

Process pints (473 ml) for 25 minutes and quarts (946 ml) for 30 minutes in pressure canner at pressure listed for your altitude and canner (see Adjust for Altitude! on page 20).

Corn

METHOD: PRESSURE CANNING

PROCESSING TIME:
PINTS (473 ML) 25 MINUTES;
QUARTS (946 ML) 30 MINUTES

YIELD: 7 QUARTS (6.6 L)

30 pounds (13.6 kg) corn on the cob

1 teaspoon salt per jar (optional)

Husk corn, cook in boiling water for 3 minutes, and cut corn kernels off cobs.

Pack into hot, sterilized jars. Add a teaspoon of salt (optional). Fill jars with boiling water, covering corn kernels. Leave a 1-inch (2.5 cm) headspace.

Remove any air bubbles. Wipe rims and secure lids.

Process pints (473 ml) for 25 minutes and quarts (946 ml) for 30 minutes in pressure canner at pressure listed for your altitude and canner (see Adjust for Altitude! on page 20).

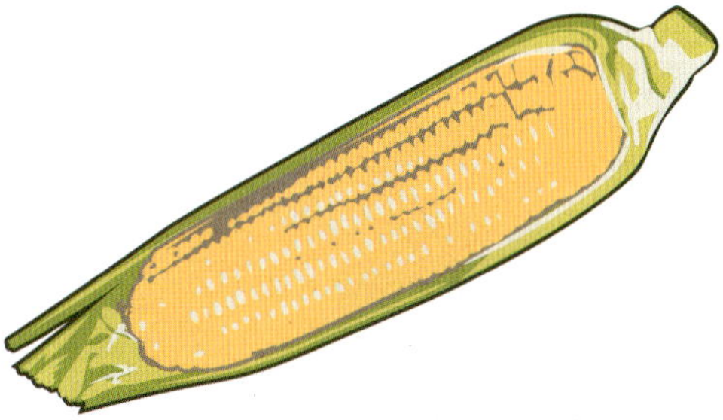

Peas, Shelled

METHOD: PRESSURE CANNING

PROCESSING TIME: 40 MINUTES

YIELD: 9 PINTS (4.3 L)

20 pounds (9.1 kg) peas, shelled

1 teaspoon salt per jar (optional)

Wash peas.

Fill hot, sterilized jars with raw peas. Add a teaspoon of salt (optional). Fill jars with boiling water, covering peas. Leave a 1-inch (2.5 cm) headspace.

Remove any air bubbles. Wipe rims and secure lids.

Process pints (473 ml) and quarts (946 ml) for 40 minutes in pressure canner at pressure listed above for your altitude and canner (see Adjust for Altitude! on page 20).

Peppers

METHOD: PRESSURE CANNING

PROCESSING TIME: 35 MINUTES

YIELD: 9 PINTS (4.3 L)

10 pounds (4.5 kg) peppers

½ teaspoon salt per jar (optional)

Blanch peppers in boiling water or blister in a broiler for 6 minutes. Place in a bowl and cover with plastic wrap or a tight-fitting plate. Let sit until cool and then remove skins. Cut to desired size.

Fill hot, sterilized jars with peppers. Add a ½ teaspoon of salt (optional). Fill jars with boiling water, covering peppers. Leave a 1-inch (2.5 cm) headspace.

Remove any air bubbles. Wipe rims and secure lids.

Process pints (473 ml) for 35 minutes in pressure canner at pressure listed for your altitude and canner (see Adjust for Altitude! on page 20).

Potatoes

METHOD: PRESSURE CANNING

PROCESSING TIME:
PINTS (473 ML) 35 MINUTES;
QUARTS (946 ML) 40 MINUTES

YIELD: 7 QUARTS (6.6 L)

20 pounds (9.1 kg) potatoes

Vitamin C (ascorbic acid) tablets, 500 mg (one tablet per gallon [3.8 L] of water)

1 teaspoon salt per jar (optional)

Wash and peel potatoes. Cut into ½- or 1-inch (1.3 or 2.5 cm) cubes.

Important: *To prevent them from darkening, place the cubed potatoes in water with an ascorbic acid solution. The easiest way to do this is to crush six 500 mg Vitamin C tablets per gallon (3.8 L) of water (see Prevent Discoloration on page 44). Keep the potatoes submerged until you are ready to cook them. Otherwise, they'll turn a very unappetizing color of gray when canned and stored.*

Transfer potatoes from ascorbic acid bath to boiling water and cook for 2 minutes.

Fill hot, sterilized jars with hot potatoes. Add a teaspoon of salt (optional). Fill jars with fresh boiling water, covering potatoes. Leave a 1-inch (2.5 cm) headspace.

Remove any air bubbles. Wipe rims and secure lids.

Process pints (473 ml) for 35 minutes and quarts (946 ml) for 40 minutes in pressure canner at pressure listed for your altitude and canner (see Adjust for Altitude! on page 20).

Squash (Winter) and Pumpkin

Select winter squash and pumpkins with a hard rind. Do not use spaghetti squash or other varieties with stringy pulp. Smaller pumpkins meant for pies (as opposed to ones used for carving jack-o'-lanterns) produce better results.

METHOD: PRESSURE CANNING

PROCESSING TIME:
PINTS (473 ML) 55 MINUTES;
QUARTS (946 ML) 90 MINUTES

YIELD: 7 QUARTS (6.6 L)

18 pounds (8.2 kg) hard winter squash or pumpkin

Wash squash/pumpkin, remove seeds, peel, and cut into 1-inch (2.5 cm) pieces.

Cook squash/pumpkin in boiling water for 2 minutes.

Pack hot, sterilized jars with cubes of squash/pumpkin. Fill jars with boiling water, covering squash/pumpkin. Leave a 1-inch (2.5 cm) headspace.

Remove any air bubbles. Wipe rims and secure lids.

Process pints (473 ml) for 55 minutes and quarts (946 ml) for 90 minutes in pressure canner at pressure listed for your altitude and canner (see Adjust for Altitude! on page 20).

Important: *Do not mash or purée squash/pumpkin prior to canning; the purée is too dense to reliably heat through. Keep the squash/pumpkin cubes intact for safe canning. To make purées or soups later, simply dump the canned squash/pumpkin cubes into a blender and mix for a few minutes.*

PREVENT DISCOLORATION

Soak light-colored produce like apples, peaches, pears, nectarines, apricots, and potatoes in an ascorbic acid solution to keep from turning brown. Powdered ascorbic acid or crushed Vitamin C tablets are the best and easiest way to prevent produce from darkening. This is a simple, but important step. Here's how:

1. Crush three 500 mg Vitamin C (ascorbic acid) tablets into 2 quarts (1.9 L) of cold water and add fruit.
2. Soak for at least 2 minutes. Keep produce in solution until you're ready to use it.

Creamed Corn

You'd be forgiven for thinking there was actual cream in this creamed corn, yet this is the perfect side dish for vegans or even the base for a creamy vegan soup.

METHOD: PRESSURE CANNING

PROCESSING TIME: 1 HOUR, 35 MINUTES

PRESSURE:
10 POUNDS (68.9 KPA)
WEIGHTED GAUGE
11 POUNDS (75.8 KPA)
DIAL GAUGE

YIELD: 3 PINTS (1.4 L)

7 pounds (3.2 kg) fresh ears of corn, husks and silks removed

1½ teaspoons canning salt

In a large pot of boiling water (or more pots as needed) over high heat, blanch the corn on the cob for 4 minutes. Remove the corn and let the cobs cool enough to handle safely.

With a sharp knife, cut the corn kernels from the cobs. Cut about ¾ of the kernel to avoid cutting into the cob. Run the back of your knife blade over the cob a second time to remove the corn "milk" and combine the "milk" with kernels.

In a large pot over high heat, combine the corn kernels with 1 cup (235 ml) of water for every 2 cups (308 g) corn–corn milk mixture. Bring the mixture to a boil.

In a separate pot over high heat, bring 2 quarts (1.9 L) water to a boil in case you need more hot liquid to top up your jars.

Using a slotted ladle or large slotted spoon, carefully ladle the corn evenly into hot, sterilized jars, leaving a bit more than 1 inch (2.5 cm) of headspace. Pour the boiling water over the top, as needed, leaving a 1-inch (2.5 cm) headspace. Add ½ teaspoon of salt to each pint (473 ml) jar.

Remove any air bubbles with a plastic or wooden utensil, adding more boiling water as needed to maintain the proper 1-inch (2.5 cm) headspace. Wipe the rims and seal the jars hand-tight with the 2-piece lids.

Carefully transfer the filled jars to the rack inside the pressure canner. Process the jars at the pressure listed above for 1 hour, 35 minutes.

Let the canner return to 0 pounds pressure (0.7 kPa). Wait 10 minutes more and then carefully open the canner lid according to the manufacturer's instructions.

With a jar lifter, remove the jars and place them on a clean dish towel away from any drafts. Allow to cool undisturbed for 12 to 24 hours and then check the seals. If any jars have not sealed properly, refrigerate them and use the corn within 2 weeks. Label the remaining jars with the recipe name and date before storing.

Corn Relish

Corn relish is a versatile condiment. It can be used like creamed corn—for a pop of summery flavor in the deep of winter. However, it's also a summer classic, found at backyard barbecues across the country. At my house, we eat it on our burgers, mixed into chicken salad, and some even take an extra spoonful or two for a bite on the side!

METHOD: PRESSURE CANNING

PROCESSING TIME: 20 MINUTES

PRESSURE: 10 POUNDS (68.9 KPA) WEIGHTED GAUGE, 11 POUNDS (75.8 KPA) DIAL GAUGE

YIELD: 6 PINTS (2.8 L)

16 to 20 fresh ears of corn, husks and silks removed

2 cups (320 g) chopped onion

1 cup (150 g) chopped green bell pepper

¾ cup (113 g) chopped red bell pepper

1½ cups (300 g) sugar

1 quart (946 ml) white or apple cider vinegar, minimum 5 percent acidity

1 tablespoon (9 g) dry mustard

1 tablespoon (11 g) mustard seeds

2 tablespoons (36 g) canning salt

With a sharp knife, cut the corn kernels from the ears until you have about 2 quarts (1.9 L) of kernels.

In large pot over high heat, combine the corn, onion, green and red bell peppers, sugar, vinegar, dry mustard, mustard seeds, and canning salt. Bring to a boil, stirring occasionally.

Once the mixture reaches a boil, stir it again, cover the pot, and simmer for 20 minutes. Continue stirring occasionally to prevent scorching.

Carefully ladle the corn mixture into hot, sterilized jars, leaving 1 inch (2.5 cm) of headspace. You should have enough relish to fill your jars and there is no recommended top-up liquid for this recipe.

Remove any air bubbles with a plastic or wooden utensil, adding more relish as needed to maintain the proper 1-inch (2.5 cm) headspace.

Wipe the rims and seal the jars hand-tight with the 2-piece lids.

Carefully transfer the filled jars to the rack inside the pressure canner. Process the jars at the pressure listed above for 20 minutes.

Let the canner return to 0 pounds pressure (0.7 kPa). Wait 10 minutes more and then carefully open the canner lid according to the manufacturer's instructions.

With a jar lifter, remove the jars and place them on a clean dish towel away from any drafts. Allow to cool undisturbed for 12 to 24 hours and then check the seals. If any jars have not sealed properly, refrigerate them and use the relish within 2 weeks. Label the remaining jars with the recipe name and date before storing.

Spicy Dilly Beans

Pickled green beans, also known as *dilly beans* in some circles, are a must-have for your pantry. They make a tangy component of bean salads, but they also work great as a condiment and as a unique topping for appetizers. Some even swear by them as a garnish for a Bloody Mary, used in place of the more traditional celery stalk. Mixing green and yellow beans adds a pop of color to the jars, but no matter the visual interest, these beans are tasty. You may not be able to make enough of them to last all year!

METHOD: PRESSURE CANNING

PROCESSING TIME: 20 MINUTES

PRESSURE: 10 POUNDS (68.9 KPA) WEIGHTED GAUGE, 11 POUNDS (75.8 KPA) DIAL GAUGE

YIELD: 4 PINTS (1.9 L)

2½ cups (570 ml) distilled white vinegar, minimum 5% acidity

2½ cups (570 ml) water

¼ cup (72 g) canning salt

2½ pounds (1.1 kg) green beans, ends trimmed; measured and cut so they leave ¼ inch (6 mm) of headspace in the jars

4 garlic cloves, peeled

4 stems fresh dill, cut in half if tall

4 dried red chile peppers

1 teaspoon cayenne pepper

1 teaspoon dill seed

In a large pot over high heat, combine the vinegar, water, and salt. Bring the mixture to a boil and cook for 1 minute. Stir well while the mixture boils to make sure the salt dissolves. Reduce the heat to maintain a simmer and keep the liquid very hot while you continue to work.

Pack the beans upright in hot, sterilized jars, leaving ¼ inch (6 mm) of headspace. Cut the beans again, as needed, to leave the ¼-inch (6 mm) headspace.

In each jar, place 1 clove garlic, 1 dill sprig, 1 dried red chile pepper, ¼ teaspoon of cayenne pepper, and ¼ teaspoon of dill seed.

Carefully ladle the hot liquid over the beans, leaving ¼-inch (6 mm) of headspace.

Remove any air bubbles with a plastic or wooden utensil, adding more hot liquid as needed to maintain the proper ¼-inch (6 mm) headspace.

Wipe the rims and seal the jars hand-tight with the 2-piece lids.

Carefully transfer the filled jars to the rack inside the pressure canner. Process the jars at the pressure listed above for 20 minutes.

Let the canner return to 0 pounds pressure (0.7 kPa). Wait 10 minutes more and then carefully open the canner lid according to the manufacturer's instructions.

With a jar lifter, remove the jars and place them on a clean dish towel away from any drafts. Allow to cool undisturbed for 12 to 24 hours and then check the seals. If any jars have not sealed properly, refrigerate them and use the beans within 2 weeks. Label the remaining jars with the recipe name and date before storing.

Green Beans

In my garden, I try to pick beans just as fast as they ripen. Fresh beans are the key to canning them and keeping a slight bite. If your beans have any bend, they will surely not be crisp after canning. While it is a dangerous mistake to switch ingredients in and out of canning recipes, for this one you have my permission to use any color string-type bean you wish. They all taste great! Use these beans as a last-minute addition to your favorite stir-fry or soup. They will add a burst of fresh flavor to any dish.

METHOD: PRESSURE CANNING

PROCESSING TIME: 20 MINUTES

PRESSURE:
10 POUNDS (68.9 KPA)
WEIGHTED GAUGE
11 POUNDS (75.8 KPA)
DIAL GAUGE

YIELD: 4 PINTS (1.9 L)

1 pound (455 g) green beans, ends trimmed and cut into 2-inch (5 cm) pieces

2 teaspoons canning salt

In a medium-size pot or kettle, bring 1 quart (946 ml) water to a boil.

While the water boils, pack the green beans into hot, sterilized jars as tightly as possible.

Pour the boiling water over the beans, leaving 1 inch (2.5 cm) of headspace.

Add ½ teaspoon of salt to each pint (473 ml) jar.

Remove any air bubbles with a plastic or wooden utensil, adding more boiling water as needed to maintain the proper 1-inch (2.5 cm) headspace.

Wipe the rims and seal the jars hand-tight with the 2-piece lids.

Carefully transfer the filled jars to the rack inside the pressure canner. Process the jars at the pressure listed above for 20 minutes.

Let the canner return to 0 pounds pressure (0.7 kPa). Wait 10 minutes more and then carefully open the canner lid according to the manufacturer's instructions.

With a jar lifter, remove the jars and place them on a clean dish towel away from any drafts. Allow to cool undisturbed for 12 to 24 hours and then check the seals. If any jars have not sealed properly, refrigerate them and use the green beans within 2 weeks. Label the remaining jars with the recipe name and date before storing.

Pickled
Beets

Spiced Pickled Beets

While beets are healthy, they can sometimes be a tough sell to picky eaters or younger eaters who complain they "taste like dirt." This recipe is sure to change minds as the beets receive a treatment of sugar, spice, and everything nice. For those who already love beets, it will be hard to eat just one. Serve them as part of an appetizer spread and watch them disappear.

METHOD: PRESSURE CANNING

PROCESSING TIME: 30 MINUTES

PRESSURE:
10 POUNDS (68.9 KPA)
WEIGHTED GAUGE
11 POUNDS (75.8 KPA)
DIAL GAUGE

YIELD: 4 PINTS (1.9 L)

4 pounds (1.8 k) firm unblemished beets, washed, trimmed, leaving the root intact as well as about 2 inches (5 cm) of the stems

3 cups (480 g) thinly sliced white onion

2 cups (400 g) sugar

2½ cups (570 ml) distilled white vinegar, minimum 5% acidity

1½ cups (355 ml) water

1 teaspoon canning salt

2 tablespoons (12 g) whole-spice pickling mix, or a mix of 1 tablespoon (11 g) mustard seeds, 1 teaspoon whole allspice berries, 1 teaspoon whole cloves, and 3 cinnamon sticks

In a large pot, combine the beets with enough water to cover. Bring to a boil over high heat. Reduce the heat to low and simmer for about 20 minutes until fork-tender.

Drain the beets and run cold water over them to stop the cooking process. When cool enough to handle, use a sharp knife to remove the skins. The skins should easily come away from the flesh. Remove the stem and root at this point as well.

Slice the beets in ¼-inch (6 mm)-thick slices and place them in a large bowl. Set the beets aside.

Rinse the pot you cooked the beets in, place it over high heat, and combine the onion, sugar, vinegar, water, salt, and pickling mix in it. Bring the mixture to a boil. Reduce the heat to low and simmer for 5 minutes.

Add the beet slices to the hot mixture and simmer for 3 minutes more. Turn off the heat and remove the cinnamon sticks. Carefully ladle the hot beet and onion mixture into hot, sterilized jars. Ladle the hot cooking liquid over the beets, leaving ½ inch (1.3 cm) of headspace.

Remove any air bubbles with a plastic or wooden utensil, adding more hot liquid as needed to maintain the proper ½-inch (1.3 cm) headspace.

Wipe the rims and seal the jars hand-tight with the 2-piece lids. Carefully transfer the filled jars to the rack inside the pressure canner. Process the jars at the pressure listed above for 30 minutes.

Let the canner return to 0 pounds pressure (0.7 kPa). Wait 10 minutes more and then carefully open the canner lid according to the manufacturer's instructions.

With a jar lifter, remove the jars and place them on a clean dish towel away from any drafts. Allow to cool undisturbed for 12 to 24 hours and then check the seals. If any jars have not sealed properly, refrigerate them and use the beets within 2 weeks. Label the remaining jars with the recipe name and date before storing.

Lentils

Lentils are a popular base for healthy soup recipes. There are also many varieties of lentil salad, from Middle Eastern preparations to American classics. Unlike most beans, lentils do not need a long soak before cooking and that means there's no need to soak them before canning either. While lentils are one of the quicker legumes to cook from scratch, there's nothing as quick as cracking open a jar of your homemade canned lentils!

METHOD: PRESSURE CANNING

PROCESSING TIME: 1 HOUR, 15 MINUTES

PRESSURE:
10 POUNDS (68.9 KPA) WEIGHTED GAUGE
11 POUNDS (75.8 KPA) DIAL GAUGE

YIELD: 3 PINTS (1.4 L)

2 cups (384 g) dried lentils

4 cups (950 ml) Vegetable Broth (page 87) or store-bought broth

1 large onion, minced

Inspect the lentils carefully and remove any foreign objects, such as small stones. Place the lentils in a large pot and add the broth and onion. Bring the pot to a boil over high heat, reduce the heat, and simmer for about 5 minutes until the lentils are partially cooked.

Carefully ladle the lentils into hot, sterilized jars, filling each jar halfway. Ladle the hot cooking liquid over the lentils, leaving 1 inch (2.5 cm) of headspace in the jars.

Remove any air bubbles with a plastic or wooden utensil, adding more hot cooking liquid as needed to maintain the proper 1-inch (2.5 cm) headspace.

Wipe the rims and seal the jars hand-tight with the 2-piece lids.

Carefully transfer the filled jars to the rack inside the pressure canner. Process the jars at the pressure listed above for 1 hour, 15 minutes.

Let the canner return to 0 pounds pressure (0.7 kPa). Wait 10 minutes more and then carefully open the canner lid according to the manufacturer's instructions.

With a jar lifter, remove the jars and place them on a clean dish towel away from any drafts. Allow to cool undisturbed for 12 to 24 hours and then check the seals. If any jars have not sealed properly, refrigerate them and use the lentils within 2 weeks. Label the remaining jars with the recipe name and date before storing.

Mixed Vegetable Medley

When I was a little girl, whenever my family had mixed vegetables, I picked out every piece of mushy carrot. Now that I make them myself, I make sure every vegetable is ripe so the whole mixture is delicious. I'm happy to say my kids don't leave any vegetable behind! One quick note: Make sure to wash and dice your vegetables to a uniform size before combining them to cook or they may not cook at the same speed. Beyond making for an easy out-of-the-jar side dish, mixed vegetables are great to have on hand for soups or as a topping for healthy grain bowls.

METHOD: PRESSURE CANNING

PROCESSING TIME: 55 MINUTES

PRESSURE:
10 POUNDS (68.9 KPA)
WEIGHTED GAUGE
11 POUNDS (75.8 KPA)
DIAL GAUGE

YIELD: 4 PINTS (1.9 L)

1 cup (180 g) chopped tomatoes

7 cups (weight will vary) total of a combination of the following, all cut to uniform sizes (see headnote):

- **Diced carrots (1-inch [2.5 cm] dice)**
- **Sweet corn**
- **Green beans, cut into 1-inch (2.5 cm) pieces**
- **Diced zucchini (1-inch [2.5 cm] dice)**
- **2 teaspoons canning salt**

In a large pot, combine the tomatoes with the 7 cups (weight will vary) of vegetables you selected and add enough water to cover. Bring the mixture to a boil over high heat and boil for 5 minutes. Stir frequently to prevent any burning or sticking on the bottom of the pot.

Carefully ladle the vegetables evenly into hot, sterilized jars. Top with the hot cooking liquid, leaving 1 inch (2.5 cm) of headspace.

Add ½ teaspoon of salt to each jar.

Remove any air bubbles with a plastic or wooden utensil, adding more hot liquid as needed to maintain the proper 1-inch (2.5 cm) headspace.

Wipe the rims and seal the jars hand-tight with the 2-piece lids.

Carefully transfer the filled jars to the rack inside the pressure canner. Process the jars at the pressure listed above for 55 minutes.

Let the canner return to 0 pounds pressure (0.7 kPa). Wait 10 minutes more and then carefully open the canner lid according to the manufacturer's instructions.

With a jar lifter, remove the jars and place them on a clean dish towel away from any drafts. Allow to cool undisturbed for 12 to 24 hours and then check the seals. If any jars have not sealed properly, refrigerate them and use the vegetables within 2 weeks. Label the remaining jars with the recipe name and date before storing.

Sweet and Spicy Ginger Carrot Coins

If you want a carrot recipe with some kick, you've come to the right place. In this recipe, the sweetness from brown sugar and orange juice marries with spicy ginger, making these carrots your new favorite finger food. I've also made this recipe with baby carrots instead of carrot coins with great results. They are fantastic for a party!

METHOD: PRESSURE CANNING

PROCESSING TIME: 30 MINUTES

PRESSURE:
10 POUNDS (68.9 KPA)
WEIGHTED GAUGE
11 POUNDS (75.8 KPA)
DIAL GAUGE

YIELD: 4 PINTS (1.9 L)

2½ pounds (1.1 kg) carrots, washed and peeled

2 cups (450 g) packed brown sugar

1 cup (235 ml) freshly squeezed orange juice (from 2 to 4 oranges)

2 cups (475 ml) water

2 pieces crystallized ginger (about 1 inch [2.5 cm] each), minced

Cut the carrots into ⅓-inch (8 mm)-thick coins or 1-inch (2.5 cm) chunks, unless you're using baby carrots, which you can process whole.

In a large saucepan over medium heat, combine the brown sugar, orange juice, water, and crystallized ginger. Cook until the sugar dissolves. Keep the syrup hot, stirring occasionally, as you continue to work. Reduce the heat if the mixture comes close to a simmer.

Pack the carrots tightly into hot, sterilized jars, leaving 1 inch (2.5 cm) of headspace.

Carefully ladle the hot syrup over the carrots. Leave 1 inch (2.5 cm) of headspace.

Remove any air bubbles with a plastic or wooden utensil, adding more hot syrup as needed to maintain the proper 1-inch (2.5 cm) headspace.

Wipe the rims and seal the jars hand-tight with the 2-piece lids.

Carefully transfer the filled jars to the rack inside the pressure canner. Process the jars at the pressure listed above for 30 minutes.

Let the canner return to 0 pounds pressure (0.7 kPa). Wait 10 minutes more and then carefully open the canner lid according to the manufacturer's instructions.

With a jar lifter, remove the jars and place them on a clean dish towel away from any drafts. Allow to cool undisturbed for 12 to 24 hours and then check the seals. If any jars have not sealed properly, refrigerate them and use the carrots within 2 weeks. Label the remaining jars with the recipe name and date before storing.

Spicy Hot Pepper Mix

It seems as though every family has at least one eater who wants—no, needs—to turn the heat up. Yet, what constitutes spicy varies not only from person to person but also family to family. My family's "hot" might seem mild to you! The nice thing about this recipe is that it can be dialed up or down when it comes to heat. Make a batch of habaneros for the capsaicin hound in your house or seed jalapeño and serrano peppers from the garden for a milder mix.

METHOD: PRESSURE CANNING

PROCESSING TIME: 15 MINUTES

PRESSURE: 10 POUNDS (68.9 KPA) WEIGHTED GAUGE, 11 POUNDS (75.8 KPA) DIAL GAUGE

YIELD: 3 PINTS (1.4 L)

3 quarts (2.8 L) assorted hot peppers

¾ cup (216 g) canning salt

5 cups (1.2 L) distilled white vinegar, minimum 5% acidity

1 cup (235 ml) water

¼ cup (50 g) sugar

2 or 3 garlic cloves, sliced

NOTE:

You may want to start this recipe the night before, as you need 12 hours to soak the peppers before canning.

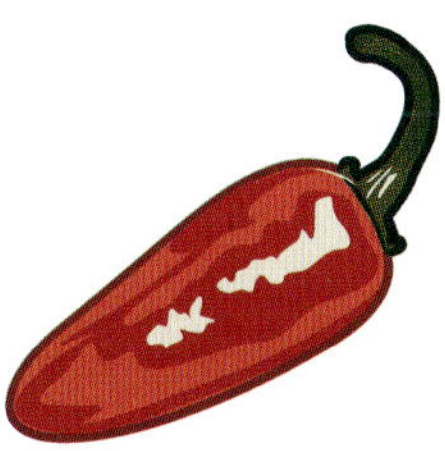

Wearing rubber gloves, wash the peppers and cut 2 slits lengthwise into each pepper.

In a very large bowl or large pot, combine the salt with 1 gallon (3.8 L) of water. Stir to dissolve the salt completely. Add the peppers and let sit for 12 hours.

Drain and rinse the peppers and pack them into hot, sterilized jars.

In a medium-size saucepan over medium heat, combine the vinegar, water, sugar, and garlic. Bring to a simmer and cook for 15 minutes. Remove and discard the garlic. Carefully pour the hot solution over the peppers, leaving a ½ inch (1.3 cm) of headspace.

Remove any air bubbles with a plastic or wooden utensil, adding more hot liquid as needed to maintain the proper ½-inch (1.3 cm) headspace.

Wipe the rims and seal the jars hand-tight with the 2-piece lids.

Carefully transfer the filled jars to the rack inside the pressure canner. Process the jars at the pressure listed above for 15 minutes.

Let the canner return to 0 pounds pressure (0.7 kPa). Wait 10 minutes more and then carefully open the canner lid according to the manufacturer's instructions.

With a jar lifter, remove the jars and place them on a clean dish towel away from any drafts. Allow to cool undisturbed for 12 to 24 hours and then check the seals. If any jars have not sealed properly, refrigerate them and use the peppers within 2 weeks. Label the remaining jars with the recipe name and date before storing.

Chapter 3

Jams, Jellies, Sauces, and Condiments

Jams are the workhorses of jelled goods. Nothing more than mashed or chopped fruit that's been lightly sweetened and jelled by pectin, they are the simplest of all to make. Jams are incredibly practical and versatile, too—use them on peanut butter and jam sandwiches, in smoothies, in hot cereal, on toast, on yogurt, on granola, on ice cream, in cookies, and in pies . . . you get the idea. With just a little preparation and planning, the options for incorporating your sauces and condiments into your favorite dishes are almost unlimited. Whether you're in the mood for a kick from your favorite chutney or craving the sweetness of a rhubarb relish—or something in between—you'll find what you need amidst this fun and delicious collection.

Simple Classic: Blueberry Jam

Here in Maine, we're fortunate that blueberries are abundant in late summer, and I never tire of this classic way to enjoy them. Blueberries require very little prep, and this jam has few ingredients, so it's easy and quick to prepare, making it an excellent choice for new jam makers. A dollop of this luscious, deep blue jam on a muffin is scrumptious—or, try it on a cracker with some extra-sharp cheddar for an unexpected flavor treat.

METHOD: BOILING WATER BATH CANNING

PROCESSING TIME: 10 MINUTES

YIELD: 4 TO 5 HALF-PINT (235 ML) JARS

2¼ pounds (1 kg) blueberries*

¼ cup (60 ml) lemon juice

2 teaspoons calcium water

1 cup (200 g) sugar

2 teaspoons Pomona's pectin powder

**Not sure how much fruit to purchase? See Measuring Up! on page 21.*

Rinse blueberries, remove stems, and mash in a large bowl.

Measure 4 cups (946 ml) of mashed blueberries (saving any extra for another use) and combine the measured quantity in a saucepan with lemon juice and calcium water. Mix well.

In a separate bowl, combine sugar and pectin powder. Mix thoroughly and set aside.

Bring blueberry mixture to a full boil over high heat. Slowly add pectin-sugar mixture, stirring constantly. Continue to stir vigorously for 1 to 2 minutes to dissolve pectin while the jam comes back up to a boil. Once the jam returns to a full boil, remove it from the heat.

Ladle hot jam into hot, sterilized jars, leaving ¼ inch (6 mm) of headspace.

Remove trapped air bubbles, wipe rims with a damp cloth, put on lids and screw bands, and tighten to fingertip tight.

Lower filled jars into water bath canner. Place lid on canner, return to a rolling boil, and process for 10 minutes (adjusting for altitude if necessary; see Adjust for Altitude! on page 20).

Remove jars with a jar lifter and allow to cool undisturbed on a clean dish towel away from any drafts for 12 to 24 hours. Confirm that jars have sealed properly. Refrigerate any jars that have not sealed and use within 2 weeks. Label the remaining jars with the recipe name and date before storing.

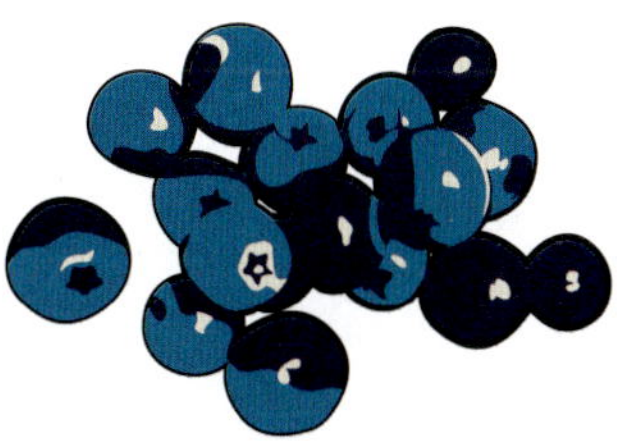

CUSTOMIZE IT!

If you're looking for something new, try spicing it up! At the same time that you add the calcium water, add up to 1 teaspoon of ground ginger, cardamom, ground cloves, cinnamon, nutmeg, or allspice. Or, you can mix and match these spices—just be sure that the total spice quantity does not exceed 1 teaspoon.

Simple Classic: Strawberry Jam

Classics are often classics for a reason, and this strawberry jam is a great example—when you're working with perfectly ripe, in-season fruit, you don't have to add much to make a spectacular jam. Use locally grown berries if you can, as their flavor and color will be richer and more vibrant than the grocery store variety. This is an excellent recipe to start with if you're new to jam making. For something different, try it warmed on top of pancakes—delicious!

METHOD: BOILING WATER BATH CANNING

PROCESSING TIME: 10 MINUTES

YIELD: 4 TO 5 HALF-PINT (235 ML) JARS

2¼ pounds (1 kg) strawberries*

2 teaspoons calcium water

1 cup (200 g) sugar

2 teaspoons Pomona's pectin powder

**Not sure how much fruit to purchase? See Measuring Up! on page 21.*

Rinse strawberries, remove stems, and mash in a large bowl.

Measure 4 cups (946 ml) of mashed strawberries (saving any extra for another use) and combine the measured quantity in a saucepan with calcium water. Mix well.

In a separate bowl, combine sugar and pectin powder. Mix thoroughly and set aside.

Bring strawberry mixture to a full boil over high heat. Slowly add pectin-sugar mixture, stirring constantly. Continue to stir vigorously for 1 to 2 minutes to dissolve pectin while the jam comes back up to a boil. Once the jam returns to a full boil, remove it from the heat.

Ladle hot jam into hot, sterilized jars, leaving 1/4 inch (6 mm) of headspace.

Remove trapped air bubbles, wipe rims with a damp cloth, put on lids and screw bands, and tighten to fingertip tight.

Lower filled jars into water bath canner. Place lid on canner, return to a rolling boil, and process for 10 minutes (adjusting for altitude if necessary; see Adjust for Altitude! on page 20).

Remove jars with a jar lifter and allow to cool undisturbed on a clean dish towel away from any drafts for 12 to 24 hours. Confirm that jars have sealed properly. Refrigerate any jars that have not sealed and use within 2 weeks. Label the remaining jars with the recipe name and date before storing.

CUSTOMIZE IT!

If you're looking for something new, why not try different fruits? In place of or in combination with the strawberry in this recipe, or in the All-Fruit Strawberry Jam (opposite) use kiwi, currant, raspberry, gooseberry, sour blackberry, sour cherry, sour plum, or canned pineapple—or use a combination of any of these fruits.

Simple Classic: Apple Jelly

Apple jelly is a fall favorite, and it's a great way to use up extra apples during apple season. Even slightly soft apples that may have been hanging around for a while will work well for this recipe, as long as they are in good condition otherwise. With your pantry stocked, you'll be able to enjoy the lovely taste of apples in this delicate, golden jelly throughout the winter months! This is an easy recipe to start with if you're new to jelly making.

METHOD: BOILING WATER BATH CANNING

PROCESSING TIME: 10 MINUTES

YIELD: 4 TO 5 HALF-PINT (235 ML) JARS

4 pounds (1.8 kg) apples*

4 cups (946 ml) water

¼ cup (60 ml) lemon juice

4 teaspoons (20 ml) calcium water

1 cup (200 g) sugar

4 teaspoons (12 g) Pomona's pectin powder

**Not sure how much fruit to purchase? See Measuring Up! on page 21.*

Peel and core apples, if desired, and then chop. Combine chopped apples in a saucepan with the 4 cups (946 ml) of water. Bring to a boil over high heat, reduce heat, and simmer, covered, for 7 to 15 minutes or until fruit is soft, stirring occasionally. Remove from heat and mash apples.

Transfer mashed fruit to a damp jelly bag or layered cheesecloth, suspend over a bowl, and allow juice to drip until dripping stops—at least 2 hours. Discard fruit pulp or save for another use.

Measure out 4 cups (946 ml) of the fruit juice and combine in a saucepan with lemon juice and calcium water.

In a separate bowl, combine sugar and pectin powder. Mix thoroughly and set aside.

Bring juice to a full boil over high heat and then slowly add pectin-sugar mixture, stirring constantly. Continue to stir vigorously for 1 to 2 minutes to dissolve pectin while the jelly comes back up to a boil. Once the jelly returns to a full boil, remove it from the heat.

Ladle hot jelly into sterilized jars, leaving ¼ inch (6 mm) of headspace.

Remove trapped air bubbles, wipe rims with a damp cloth, put on lids and screw bands, and tighten to fingertip tight.

Lower filled jars into water bath canner. Place lid on canner, return to a rolling boil, and process for 10 minutes (adjusting for altitude if necessary; see Adjust for Altitude! on page 20).

Remove jars with a jar lifter and allow to cool undisturbed on a clean dish towel away from any drafts for 12 to 24 hours. Confirm that jars have sealed properly. Refrigerate any jars that have not sealed and use within 2 weeks. Label the remaining jars with the recipe name and date before storing.

CUSTOMIZE IT!

If you're looking for something new, why not try honey instead of sugar? In place of the sugar in this recipe, use ½ to 1 cup (170 to 340 g) honey.

Simple Classic: Raspberry Jelly

This dramatic, deep-red jelly is the essence of raspberry, intensified in a jar, and it's nothing short of amazing. It's also an easy recipe to start with if you're new to jelly making. Raspberries are precious, and jelly requires a lot of them, but if you're a true raspberry lover, the results will be worth it. Spread it on a piece of pound cake, layer it with some fresh fruit and whipped cream, or turn it into a trifle if you're really feeling fancy.

METHOD: BOILING WATER BATH CANNING

PROCESSING TIME: 10 MINUTES

YIELD: 4 TO 5 HALF-PINT (235 ML) JARS

4 pounds (1.8 kg) raspberries*

⅓ cup (80 ml) water

4 teaspoons (20 ml) calcium water

1½ cups (300 g) sugar

4 teaspoons (12 g) Pomona's pectin powder

**Not sure how much fruit to purchase? See Measuring Up! on page 21.*

CUSTOMIZE IT!

If you're looking for something new, why not try different fruits? In place of or in combination with the raspberry in this recipe, use sour blackberry, currant, or strawberry—or use a combination of any of these fruits.

Carefully pick through raspberries, removing stems and any damaged parts. Rinse raspberries only if necessary. Combine in a saucepan with the ⅓ cup (80 ml) of water. Bring to a boil over high heat, reduce heat, and simmer, covered, for 1 to 2 minutes, stirring occasionally. Remove from heat and mash raspberries.

Transfer mashed fruit to a damp jelly bag or layered cheesecloth, suspend over a bowl, and allow juice to drip until dripping stops—at least 2 hours. Discard fruit pulp or save for another use.

Measure 4 cups (946 ml) of the juice and combine in a saucepan with calcium water.

In a separate bowl, combine sugar and pectin powder. Mix thoroughly and set aside.

Bring the juice mixture to a full boil over high heat and then slowly add pectin-sugar mixture, stirring constantly. Continue to stir vigorously for 1 to 2 minutes to dissolve pectin while the jelly comes back up to a boil. Once the jelly returns to a full boil, remove it from the heat.

Ladle hot jelly into sterilized jars, leaving ¼ inch (6 mm) of headspace.

Remove trapped air bubbles, wipe rims with a damp cloth, put on lids and screw bands, and tighten to fingertip tight.

Lower filled jars into water bath canner. Place lid on canner, return to a rolling boil, and process for 10 minutes (adjusting for altitude if necessary; see Adjust for Altitude! on page 20).

Remove jars with a jar lifter and allow to cool undisturbed on a clean dish towel away from any drafts for 12 to 24 hours. Confirm that jars have sealed properly. Refrigerate any jars that have not sealed and use within 2 weeks. Label the remaining jars with the recipe name and date before storing.

Stewed Tomatoes

METHOD: PRESSURE CANNING

PROCESSING TIME: PINTS (473 ML) 15 MINUTES; QUARTS (946 ML) 20 MINUTES

PRESSURE:
10 POUNDS (68.9 KPA) WEIGHTED GAUGE
11 POUNDS (75.8 KPA) DIAL GAUGE

YIELD: ABOUT 3 PINTS (473 ML)

2 quarts (1.9 L) chopped tomatoes

¼ cup (38 g) chopped green bell peppers

¼ cup (40 g) chopped onions

2 teaspoons celery salt

2 teaspoons sugar

¼ teaspoon salt

Combine ingredients, cover, and cook 10 minutes, stirring often.

Pour hot into hot, sterilized pint (473 ml) or quart (946 ml) jars, leaving a ½-inch (1.3 cm) headspace.

Remove any air bubbles with a bubble freer (see below), wipe jar rims, and adjust lids.

Process pints (473 ml) for 15 minutes and quarts (946 ml) for 20 minutes.

With a jar lifter, remove the jars and place them on a clean dish towel away from any drafts. Allow to cool undisturbed for 12 to 24 hours and then check the seals. If any jars have not sealed properly, refrigerate them and use within 2 weeks. Label the remaining jars with the recipe name and date before storing.

—Adapted from the Clemson University Extension Service website

WHAT IS A BUBBLE FREER?

The bubble freer spatula is a long tool made of heat-resistant plastic that you use to remove air bubbles in a jar before sealing. You work the tool up and down the insides of the jar and around, releasing trapped bubbles.

Tomato Catsup

METHOD: BOILING WATER BATH CANNING

PROCESSING TIME: 15 MINUTES

YIELD: 6 TO 7 PINTS

24 pounds (10.9 kg) ripe tomatoes

3 cups (480 g) onions, chopped

¾ teaspoon cayenne pepper

4 teaspoons (8 g) whole cloves

2 sticks cinnamon, crushed into small pieces under a knife handle

1½ teaspoons whole allspice berries

2 tablespoons (13 g) celery seeds

3 cups (700 ml) vinegar, minimum 5 percent acidity

1½ cups (300 g) sugar

¼ cup (72 g) canning or pickling salt

Wash tomatoes. Dip in boiling water for 30 to 60 seconds or until skins split. Then, dip in cold water, slip off skins, and remove cores. Quarter tomatoes and place in a 4-gallon (15.2 L) pot.

Add onions. Bring to boil and simmer 20 minutes, uncovered.

Combine spices in a spice bag. Place spices in a spice bag and vinegar in a 2-quart (1.9 L) saucepan. Bring to boil. Cover, turn off heat, and let stand for 20 minutes.

Remove spice bag from the vinegar and add the vinegar to the tomato mixture. Boil about 30 minutes.

Press boiled mixture through a food mill or sieve. Return to the pot. Add sugar and salt and boil gently, stirring frequently until volume is reduced by one-half or until mixture rounds up on spoon without separation.

Pour into hot, sterilized pint (473 ml) jars, leaving a ⅛-inch (3 mm) headspace.

Remove any air bubbles. Wipe jar rims. Adjust lids.

Process 15 minutes in a boiling water canner.

With a jar lifter, remove the jars and place them on a clean dish towel away from any drafts. Allow to cool undisturbed for 12 to 24 hours and then check the seals. If any jars have not sealed properly, refrigerate them and use within 2 weeks. Label the remaining jars with the recipe name and date before storing.

—Adapted from the National Center for Home Food Preservation (NCHFP) website

Tomato Jam

1½ pounds (680 g) tomatoes

6 tablespoons (90 ml) bottled lemon juice

1-inch (2.5 cm) piece of fresh ginger

Peel and slice ripe tomatoes, put them with an equal weight of sugar, and boil an hour with 6 tablespoons (90 ml) of bottled lemon juice per every 1½ pounds (680 g) of tomatoes and an equal measure of water to fruit.

Tie ginger enough to flavor to taste (about 1-inch [2.5 cm] slice per 1½ pounds [680 g]) in a thin muslin bag and add to the jam before it is done, about 30 minutes.

When it passes the jelly test (see below), remove the ginger and skim.

Pack hot in hot, sterilized jars and store immediately in refrigerator, using up within a week.

Green Tomato Jam

6 pounds (2.7 kg) green tomatoes

4 pounds (1.8 kg) sugar

1 cup (235 ml) water

2 ounces (55 g) grated fresh ginger

Slice tomatoes thin, mix with remaining ingredients, and simmer slowly for 3 hours.

Strain through a coarse strainer.

Pack hot in hot, sterilized jars, seal, and store immediately in refrigerator.

SHEET OR SPOON TEST: ALSO KNOWN AS THE JELLY TEST

Dip a cool, metal spoon into the boiling jelly mixture. Raise the spoon about 12 inches (30 cm) above the pan, out of the steam. Turn the spoon so the liquid runs off the side. When the mixture first starts to boil, the drops will be light and syrupy. As the syrup continues to boil, the drops will become heavier and will drop off the spoon two at a time. The jelly is done when the syrup forms two drops that flow together and sheet, or hang off, the edge of the spoon.

USING BOTTLED LEMON JUICE

When lemon or lime juice is listed in a recipe, you should use the bottled version rather than fresh unless specified. Yes, you read that right. I know this may come as a surprise, and frankly it's one of those things about canning that I personally find a bit challenging, but there is a very good reason for doing it this way. Bottled lemon juice and lime juice have a standard level of acidity, whereas the acidity levels of fresh lemons and fresh limes vary. Because acidity plays such an important role in jam making, it's necessary to add the proper amount, making bottled your safest option.

Tomato Salsa

METHOD: BOILING WATER BATH CANNING

PROCESSING TIME: 35 MINUTES

YIELD: 5 PINTS (2.4 L)

10 cups (1.8 kg) tomatoes, peeled, cored, and diced

1 cup (150 g) chopped green bell pepper

2 cups (320 g) chopped onions

½ cup (72 g) chopped hot peppers (a mixture of banana and jalapeño peppers with seeds removed)

Add diced tomatoes to large, stainless steel or enamel pot and cook for 30 minutes until tomatoes are very soft and the large chunks are gone.

Using a large spoon or cup, remove excess liquid from the pot and then add remaining ingredients (except lemon juice).

Continue to cook at a low boil for 20 minutes, stirring frequently.

Using a funnel, fill hot, sterilized canning jars, leaving a ½-inch (1.3 cm) of headspace. Add a tablespoon (15 ml) of lemon juice to each jar. Remove any air bubbles with a rubber spatula or skewer.

Clean rims and any spills with sterile cloth. Secure lids and rings.

Process in a boiling water bath canner for 35 minutes, adjusting for altitude if necessary (see Adjust for Altitude! on page 20).

Use a jar lifter to remove the jars and let cool undisturbed on a clean dish towel away from any drafts. Check the seals after 12 to 24 hours. Refrigerate any unsealed jars and use within 2 weeks. Label the remaining jars with the recipe name and date before storing.

Lemongrass Syrup

There are hundreds of ways to use this versatile syrup. Try ladling it over cakes or fruit salads or adding a tablespoon (15 ml) per glass to iced tea or lemonade.

METHOD: BOILING WATER BATH CANNING

PROCESSING TIME: 20 MINUTES

YIELD: 4 PINTS (1.9 L)

3 cups (600 g) sugar

3 cups (700 ml) water

3 cups (700 ml) white grape juice

8 lemongrass stalks (core only), sliced

4 lemongrass stalks (core only), cut to 3-inch (7.5 cm) pieces

In a saucepan, combine sugar, water, grape juice, and lemongrass slices and pieces. Simmer over medium heat for 10 minutes, stirring frequently.

Using tongs, remove lemongrass stalk pieces from syrup and place into hot, sterilized canning jars.

Strain syrup to remove lemongrass slices. Pour into jars, leaving a ½-inch (1.3 cm) headspace.

Remove any air bubbles. Wipe rims and secure lids.

Process for 20 minutes in a boiling water bath canner, adjusting for altitude if necessary (see Adjust for Altitude! on page 20).

Use a jar lifter to remove the jars and let cool undisturbed on a clean dish towel away from any drafts. Check the seals after 12 to 24 hours. Refrigerate any unsealed jars and use within 2 weeks. Label the remaining jars with the recipe name and date before storing.

Below are 3 fun cocktail ideas using lemongrass syrup.

LEMONGRASS MOJITO

In a cocktail shaker, combine 4 sprigs of fresh mint with a tablespoon (15 ml) of lemongrass syrup. Muddle mint and syrup (you can use the back of a spoon). Add a jigger (44 ml) of rum and ½ cup (4 cubes) of ice. Shake and pour all into a tall glass. Top with club soda. Garnish with a small stalk of lemongrass.

LEMONGRASS GIN FIZZ

In a cocktail shaker, mix a tablespoon (15 ml) of lemongrass syrup, ¼ teaspoon of lime juice, and a jigger (44 ml) of gin. Shake and pour into a cocktail glass. Top with either tonic water or ginger ale. Garnish with a lime wedge.

SIMPLE RUM SIPPER

In a highball, mix a tablespoon (15 ml) of lemongrass syrup with a jigger (44 ml) of rum and juice from a fresh lime. Add ice and top with club soda for a refreshing cocktail.

Mango Chutney

This makes a great side with many meals. We've toned down the spices in this recipe—if you like it fiery hot, simply add more cayenne pepper!

METHOD: BOILING WATER BATH CANNING

PROCESSING TIME: 15 MINUTES

YIELD: 8 HALF-PINT (1.9 L) JARS

9 pounds (4.1 kg) green mangoes, peeled, pitted, and sliced (see sidebar below)

1 cup (200 g) sugar

1 cup (235 ml) grape juice

2 cups (475 ml) cider vinegar, minimum 5 percent acidity

2 medium onions, chopped

2 red bell peppers, chopped

1 cup (145 g) raisins

1 tablespoon (18 g) salt

1½ teaspoons fresh ginger, finely chopped

¼ teaspoon cayenne pepper

1 teaspoon dry mustard

1 teaspoon ground cinnamon

1 tablespoon (7 g) ground cloves

2 garlic cloves, minced

Juice from 2 limes, plus zest

Place mango slices flat on a baking sheet. Sprinkle with 2 teaspoons of salt. Set aside for 8 to 12 hours (this removes the excess liquid).

Add sugar, grape juice, and vinegar to a saucepan or stockpot. Bring to a boil and then reduce to simmer.

Dice mangoes.

Add mangoes and remaining ingredients to saucepan or stockpot. Simmer for 30 to 45 minutes, stirring often.

Ladle into hot, sterilized half-pint (235 ml) jars, leaving a ¼-inch (6 mm) headspace.

Remove any air bubbles. Wipe rims and secure lids.

Process in a boiling water bath canner for 15 minutes, adjusting for altitude if necessary (see Adjust for Altitude! on page 20).

Use a jar lifter to remove the jars and let cool undisturbed on a clean dish towel away from any drafts. Check the seals after 12 to 24 hours. Refrigerate any unsealed jars and use within 2 weeks. Label the remaining jars with the recipe name and date before storing.

MANGO MADNESS!

Mangoes can be maddening if you don't know how to prepare themTo cut up a mango with ease, hold the mango upright and starting from the top, slice down along one of the flat sides of the mango, cutting close along the flat side of the pit, slicing off as much flesh as possible. Then, repeat the process on the opposite flat side of the mango. Gently score the flesh of each of the sliced-off sides of the mango in a grid pattern and then push the skins inside out and carefully slice the mango cubes off the skins. Also, slice off and cut up any flesh remaining on the pit before discarding skins and pit.

Nectarine-Raspberry Preserves

These preserves can be eaten alone or used to make a fruit crisp, pie, or bars.

METHOD: BOILING WATER BATH CANNING

PROCESSING TIME:
PINTS (473 ML) 30 MINUTES;
QUARTS (946 ML) 35 MINUTES

YIELD: 4 QUARTS (3.8 L)

10 pounds (4.5 kg) nectarines, peeled and cut into bite-sized pieces

1 quart (946 ml) plus 6 cups (1.4 L) water, divided

3 Vitamin C tablets (500 mg each)

4 cups (946 ml) apple or white grape juice

2 cups (475 ml) water

½ cup (100 g) sugar

3 pounds (1.4 kg) raspberries, washed

Soak nectarines in a solution of 1 quart (946 ml) of water mixed with 3 crushed Vitamin C tablets for 2 to 3 minutes to prevent discoloration. Leave fruit in solution until ready to use.

Heat 6 cups (1.4 L) of water, apple or white grape juice, and sugar to a simmer. Add nectarines and cook for 5 minutes.

Use a slotted spoon to move nectarines from pan. Place in sterilized quart (946 ml) jars. Add raspberries to jars. Fill with hot syrup. Add more boiling water if necessary, leaving a ½-inch (1.3 cm) headspace.

Remove any air bubbles. Wipe rims and secure lids.

Process in a boiling water bath canner: 30 minutes for pints (473 ml) and 35 minutes for quarts (946 ml), adjusting for altitude if necessary (see Adjust for Altitude! on page 20).

Use a jar lifter to remove the jars and let cool undisturbed on a clean dish towel away from any drafts. Check the seals after 12 to 24 hours. Refrigerate any unsealed jars and use within 2 weeks. Label the remaining jars with the recipe name and date before storing.

Taco Sauce

Our version of Mexican night is pretty tame by most standards, but we love the slightly spicy taste of this recipe. Use it with the ground meat of your choice or get creative: I've found I can get as many vegetables as I want into my kids when I flavor them with this sauce. That said, it's not authentic. If you are a purist, be forewarned!

METHOD: PRESSURE CANNING

PROCESSING TIME: 15 MINUTES

PRESSURE:
10 POUNDS (68.9 KPA)
WEIGHTED GAUGE
11 POUNDS (75.8 KPA)
DIAL GAUGE

YIELD: 4 PINTS (1.9 L)

8 cups (1.4 kg) peeled, chopped, and drained tomatoes,

1 medium-size onion, chopped

1 cup (100 g) chopped scallion

½ cup (72 g) chopped seeded jalapeño peppers, or other green chile

4 garlic cloves, chopped

1 teaspoon salt

1 teaspoon chili powder

½ teaspoon ground cumin

In a saucepan over medium heat, combine the tomatoes, onion, scallion, jalapeños, garlic, salt, chili powder, and cumin. Stir to combine and bring to a simmer. Simmer for 30 minutes, stirring frequently.

Strain the sauce through a fine-mesh strainer and return it to the pan. Bring the sauce to a boil and cook for 5 minutes.

Carefully ladle the hot sauce into hot, sterilized jars, leaving 1 inch (2.5 cm) of headspace.

Remove any air bubbles with a plastic or wooden utensil, adding more hot sauce as needed to maintain the proper 1-inch (2.5 cm) headspace.

Wipe the rims and seal the jars hand-tight with the 2-piece lids.

Carefully transfer the filled jars to the rack inside the pressure canner. Process the jars at the pressure listed above for 15 minutes.

Let the canner return to 0 pounds pressure (0.7 kPa). Wait 10 minutes more and then carefully open the canner lid according to the manufacturer's instructions.

With a jar lifter, remove the jars and place them on a clean dish towel away from any drafts. Allow to cool undisturbed for 12 to 24 hours and then check the seals. If any jars have not sealed properly, refrigerate them and use the sauce within 2 weeks. Label the remaining jars with the recipe name and date before storing.

Peach Tomato Salsa

While I normally advocate only the freshest fruits and vegetables when canning, this salsa is an exception. It is a wonderful way to use peaches that aren't quite ripe. As with most fruit salsas, this is a great condiment not only for tacos, but for fish and chicken as well.

METHOD: PRESSURE CANNING

PROCESSING TIME: 10 MINUTES

PRESSURE:
10 POUNDS (68.9 KPA)
WEIGHTED GAUGE
11 POUNDS (75.8 KPA)
DIAL GAUGE

YIELD: 6 PINTS (2.8 L)

2 pounds (900 g) paste-type tomatoes, such as Roma

3 pounds (1.4 kg) peaches, chopped

2½ cups (400 g) chopped onion

2 cups (300 g) chopped green bell pepper

2 cups (300 g) chopped peeled apple

1 tablespoon (18 g) salt

1 teaspoon red pepper flakes

3¾ cups (845 g) packed light brown sugar

2¼ cups (535 ml) apple cider vinegar, minimum 5 percent acidity

¼ cup (25 g) pickling spice, tied in a muslin bag

Prepare an ice-water bath and bring a large saucepan of water to a boil.

REMOVE THE TOMATO SKINS: Working 1 tomato at a time for best results, place the tomato into the boiling water for 1 minute. Transfer to the ice-water bath. The skins will split and peel off easily. Chop the peeled tomatoes.

Empty the pan and return it to medium-high heat. In it, combine the tomatoes, peaches, onion, green bell pepper, apple, salt, red pepper flakes, brown sugar, vinegar, and the muslin bag containing the pickling spices.

As the mixture starts to warm, stir to incorporate everything. Bring the mixture to a boil, stirring frequently to keep it from burning. Once the mixture boils, reduce the heat to low, and simmer for 30 minutes.

Remove and discard the muslin bag and turn off the heat.

Carefully ladle the salsa into hot, sterilized jars, leaving ½ inch (1.3 cm) of headspace.

Remove any air bubbles with a plastic or wooden utensil, adding more hot salsa as needed to maintain the proper ½-inch (1.3 cm) headspace.

Wipe the rims and seal the jars hand-tight with the 2-piece lids.

Carefully transfer the filled jars to the rack inside the pressure canner. Process the jars at the pressure listed above for 10 minutes.

Let the canner return to 0 pounds pressure (0.7 kPa). Wait 10 minutes more and then carefully open the canner lid according to the manufacturer's instructions.

With a jar lifter, remove the jars and place them on a clean dish towel away from any drafts. Allow to cool undisturbed for 12 to 24 hours and then check the seals. If any jars have not sealed properly, refrigerate them and use the salsa within 1 week. Label the remaining jars with the recipe name and date before storing.

Tomatillo Salsa

For a change of pace, I like to make and serve this green, not-so-spicy salsa for everyday eating. If you're unfamiliar with tomatillo salsa, it is quite a departure from a classic red tomato salsa. The tomatillos have a unique flavor to start—tart, fruity, and slightly herbal. Throw in a good amount of vinegar and cilantro and you end up with a bright, fresh flavor. Use it as you would any salsa, as a dip or a topping for tacos. Or, try a recipe that features tomatillo salsa, such as enchiladas verde.

METHOD: PRESSURE CANNING

PROCESSING TIME: 15 MINUTES

PRESSURE:
10 POUNDS (68.9 KPA)
WEIGHTED GAUGE
11 POUNDS (75.8 KPA)
DIAL GAUGE

YIELD: 2 PINTS (946 ML)

2 pounds (900 g) tomatillos, cleaned, cored, and diced into small pieces

1 large onion, roughly chopped

4 large Anaheim chiles, seeded

4 garlic cloves, peeled

1 cup (235 ml) distilled white vinegar, minimum 5 percent acidity

¼ cup (60 ml) freshly squeezed lime juice (from about 2 limes)

2 tablespoons (2g) minced fresh cilantro leaves

2 teaspoons ground cumin

½ teaspoon canning salt

½ teaspoon red pepper flakes

Place the tomatillos in a large pot.

In a food processor, combine the onion, chiles, and garlic. Pulse a few times until the vegetables are broken into very small pieces. Add them to the tomatillos. Bring the mixture to a boil over high heat.

As the mixture starts to warm, add the vinegar, lime juice, cilantro, cumin, canning salt, and red pepper flakes. Stir well to incorporate the ingredients. Once the salsa boils, reduce the heat to low and simmer for 10 minutes.

Carefully ladle the hot salsa into hot, sterilized jars, leaving 1 inch (2.5 cm) of headspace.

Remove any air bubbles with a plastic or wooden utensil, adding more hot salsa as needed to maintain the proper 1-inch (2.5 cm) headspace.

Wipe the rims and seal the jars hand-tight with the 2-piece lids.

Carefully transfer the filled jars to the rack inside the pressure canner. Process the jars at the pressure listed above for 15 minutes.

Let the canner return to 0 pounds pressure (0.7 kPa). Wait 10 minutes more and then carefully open the canner lid according to the manufacturer's instructions.

With a jar lifter, remove the jars and place them on a clean dish towel away from any drafts. Allow to cool undisturbed for 12 to 24 hours and then check the seals. If any jars have not sealed properly, refrigerate them and use the salsa within 2 weeks. Label the remaining jars with the recipe name and date before storing.

Green Tomato Chutney

No matter how early I plant my tomatoes, I always end up with plenty that don't have a hint of red on them by first frost. I used to be upset by these stragglers until I found recipes like this that put green tomatoes to good use. Now, I'm actually quite happy if there are plenty of green tomatoes remaining at the end of gardening season.

METHOD: PRESSURE CANNING

PROCESSING TIME: 10 MINUTES

PRESSURE:
10 POUNDS (68.9 KPA)
WEIGHTED GAUGE
11 POUNDS (75.8 KPA)
DIAL GAUGE

YIELD: 4 PINTS (1.9 L)

10 paste-type tomatoes, such as Roma

2 onions, chopped

2 green bell peppers, seeded and chopped

2 garlic cloves, minced

2 chile peppers, such as Thai chiles, seeded and chopped (or include the seeds for more heat)

1 jalapeño pepper, seeded and chopped (or include the seeds for more heat)

¼ cup (60 ml) freshly squeezed lemon juice (from about 2 lemons)

1 tablespoon (18 g) salt

1 teaspoon freshly ground black pepper

2 tablespoons (2 g) chopped fresh cilantro leaves

Prepare an ice-water bath and bring a large pot of water to a boil.

Remove the tomato skins: Working 1 tomato at a time for best results, place the tomato into the boiling water for 1 minute. Transfer to the ice-water bath. The skins will split and peel off easily. Chop the peeled tomatoes.

Empty the pot and return it to medium-high heat. In it, combine the tomatoes, onions, green bell pepper, garlic, chile and jalapeño peppers, lemon juice, salt, black pepper, and cilantro. Stir to combine. Bring the mixture to a boil. Reduce the heat to low and simmer for 15 minutes, stirring frequently.

Carefully ladle the hot chutney into hot, sterilized jars, leaving ¾ inch (1.9 cm) of headspace.

Remove any air bubbles with a plastic or wooden utensil, adding more hot chutney as needed to maintain the proper ¾-inch (1.9 cm) headspace.

Wipe the rims and seal the jars hand-tight with the 2-piece lids.

Carefully transfer the filled jars to the rack inside the pressure canner. Process the jars at the pressure listed above for 10 minutes.

Let the canner return to 0 pounds pressure (0.7 kPa). Wait 10 minutes more and then carefully open the canner lid according to the manufacturer's instructions.

With a jar lifter, remove the jars and place them on a clean dish towel away from any drafts. Allow to cool undisturbed for 12 to 24 hours and then check the seals. If any jars have not sealed properly, refrigerate them and use the chutney within 2 weeks. Label the remaining jars with the recipe name and date before storing.

Barbecue Sauce

Every spring, we break out the grill long before the last snow. It must be funny to see us gathered around a smoking grill in our winter coats! With such a strong urge to grill, it's no surprise we use more barbecue sauce than the average family. I have to put up quite a bit so we don't run out.

METHOD: PRESSURE CANNING

PROCESSING TIME: 15 MINUTES

PRESSURE:
10 POUNDS (68.9 KPA)
WEIGHTED GAUGE
11 POUNDS (75.8 KPA)
DIAL GAUGE

YIELD: 2 PINTS (946 ML)

2 quarts (1.9 L) Roma tomatoes

1 cup (160 g) chopped onion

1 green bell pepper, seeded and chopped

1 hot pepper, such as jalapeño or serrano, seeded and minced

1 garlic clove, minced

½ cup (115 g) packed dark brown sugar

1½ teaspoons smoked paprika

1½ teaspoons salt

½ cup (120 ml) plus 2 tablespoons (28 ml) white or apple cider vinegar, minimum 5 percent acidity

Prepare an ice-water bath and bring a large saucepan of water to a boil.

Remove the tomato skins: Working 1 tomato at a time for best results, place the tomato into the boiling water for 1 minute. Transfer to the ice-water bath. The skins will split and peel off easily. Chop the peeled tomatoes.

In a large stockpot over medium heat, combine the chopped tomatoes, onion, green bell pepper, hot pepper, garlic, brown sugar, smoked paprika, salt, and vinegar. Cook for about 30 minutes until the vegetables are very soft.

Remove the pot from the heat and use an immersion blender or food mill to purée the sauce as much as possible. Strain the sauce through a fine-mesh to remove any large pieces. At this point, you should have a nice smooth sauce. Return the sauce to the heat and simmer until it has reduced by half, about 45 minutes.

Carefully ladle the hot barbecue sauce into hot, sterilized jars, leaving ½ inch (1.3 cm) of headspace.

Remove any air bubbles with a plastic or wooden utensil, adding more hot barbecue sauce as needed to maintain the proper ½-inch (1.3 cm) headspace.

Wipe the rims and seal the jars hand-tight with the 2-piece lids.

Carefully transfer the filled jars to the rack inside the pressure canner. Process the jars at the pressure listed above for 15 minutes.

Let the canner return to 0 pounds pressure (0.7 kPa). Wait 10 minutes more and then carefully open the canner lid according to the manufacturer's instructions.

With a jar lifter, remove the jars and place them on a clean dish towel away from any drafts. Allow to cool undisturbed for 12 to 24 hours and then check the seals. If any jars have not sealed properly, refrigerate them and use the barbecue sauce within 2 weeks. Label the remaining jars with the recipe name and date before storing.

Pepper Relish

METHOD: BOILING WATER BATH CANNING

PROCESSING TIME: 5 MINUTES

YIELD: 9 HALF-PINT (235 ML) JARS

3 cups (450 g) red bell peppers, finely chopped

3 cups (450 g) green bell peppers, finely chopped

6 cups (960 g) onions, finely chopped

6 cups (1.4 L) vinegar, minimum 5 percent acidity

1½ cups (300 g) sugar

2 tablespoons (36 g) canning or pickling salt

Combine all together in a large pot and boil gently until thick and reduced by one-half.

Pack hot into hot, sterilized half-pint (235 ml) or pint (473 ml) jars, leaving ½ inch (1.3 cm) of headspace.

Remove any air bubbles. Wipe rims and secure lids.

Process for 5 minutes in a boiling water bath canner.

With a jar lifter, remove the jars and place them on a clean dish towel away from any drafts. Allow to cool undisturbed for 12 to 24 hours and then check the seals. If any jars have not sealed properly, refrigerate them and use within 2 weeks. Label the remaining jars with the recipe name and date before storing.

—Adapted from the NCHFP website

Rhubarb Relish

This relish is delicious with meats.

¼ pound (55 g) raisins, chopped

½ pound (115 g) dates, chopped

3 cups (700 ml) vinegar, minimum 5 percent acidity

2 pounds (900 g) rhubarb

2 pounds (900 g) brown sugar

2 teaspoons ground ginger

1 tablespoon (18 g) canning or pickling salt

½ cup (60 g) walnuts, chopped

Cover raisins and dates with vinegar in a nonreactive bowl and let stand about an hour.

Wash rhubarb and cut in short lengths.

Combine raisin, date, and vinegar mixture with all ingredients except nuts.

Cook slowly until thick and clear—about 2 hours, stirring frequently.

Add nuts, cook 10 minutes longer.

Pack hot in hot, sterilized pint (473 ml) jars, seal, and store immediately in refrigerator.

—Mrs. D. C., Iowa

Wild Gooseberry Relish

5 cups (750 g) wild gooseberries

1½ pounds (680 g) raisins

1 medium onion

3 tablespoons (54 g) salt

1 quart (946 ml) vinegar, minimum 5 percent acidity

1 cup (225 g) brown sugar

3 tablespoons (27 g) dry mustard

3 tablespoons (17 g) ground ginger

¼ teaspoon cayenne pepper

1 tablespoon (7 g) turmeric

Pick over, wash, and stem gooseberries.

Chop raisins and onion and add to gooseberries.

Place in kettle, add remaining ingredients, bring slowly to a boil, and simmer gently 45 minutes.

Strain through a coarse sieve.

Pack hot in hot, sterilized pint (473 ml) jars. Seal and store immediately in refrigerator.

Apple Indian Chutney

This is a hot, delicious sauce.

6 pounds (2.7 kg) sour apples, peeled, cored, and chopped fine

2 lemons, chopped fine, peel and all, seeds removed

2 cups (290 g) raisins, chopped fine

2 hot green peppers

1 large onion, chopped

2 pounds (900 g) brown sugar

1 tablespoon (11 g) mustard seeds

1 tablespoon (6 g) ground ginger

½ tablespoon canning or pickling salt

3 cups (700 ml) vinegar, minimum 5 percent acidity

Mix apple with lemon to keep from turning dark.

Remove seeds from peppers and chop.

Combine all ingredients.

Bring to a boil and cook slowly until apples are tender.

Pack hot in hot, sterilized pint (473 ml) jars, seal, and store immediately in refrigerator.

Chapter 4

Stocks, Broths, Soups, and Stews

Stocks and soups fill my pantry. They're great for saving lots of money and getting fast, healthy meals on the table in minutes. This section provides recipes for some of the basics and soups with more variations and different flavors.

Chicken or Beef Stock

METHOD: PRESSURE CANNING

PROCESSING TIME:
PINTS (473 ML) 20 MINUTES
QUARTS (946 ML) 25 MINUTES

PRESSURE: BASED ON MANUFACTURER'S INSTRUCTIONS AND CANNING ALTITUDE

YIELD: 6 PINTS OR 3 QUARTS (2.8 L)

- 3 pounds (1.4 kg) of chicken pieces or 6 pounds (2.7 kg) meaty beef bones
- 3 quarts (2.8 L) water
- 2 stalks celery, diced
- 2 onions, quartered
- 2 leeks (optional, but adds a nice flavor)
- 4 garlic cloves, chopped
- 12 whole black peppercorns
- 2 bay leaves
- 1½ tablespoons (27 g) salt

In a large stainless steel or enamel pot, combine all ingredients. Bring to a boil and then reduce heat and simmer for 2½ hours.

Remove chicken pieces or beef bones (reserve chicken for another use) and strain stock through a colander or sieve lined with cheesecloth.

Let cool and skim fat.

Return stock to a boil.

Ladle stock into hot, sterilized jars. Leave a 1-inch (2.5 cm) headspace.

Remove any air bubbles. Wipe rims and secure lids.

Process pints (473 ml) for 20 minutes and quarts (946 ml) for 25 minutes at pressure listed for your altitude and canner (see Adjust for Altitude! on page 20).

Use a jar lifter to remove the jars place them on a clean dish towel away from any drafts. Let cool undisturbed for 12 to 24 hours and then check the seals. Store any unsealed jars in the refrigerator and consume within 2 weeks. Label the remaining jars with the recipe name and date before storing.

Vegetable Stock

METHOD: PRESSURE CANNING

PROCESSING TIME: PINTS (473 ML) 30 MINUTES; QUARTS (946 ML) 35 MINUTES

PRESSURE: BASED ON MANUFACTURER'S INSTRUCTIONS AND CANNING ALTITUDE

YIELD: 8 PINTS OR 4 QUARTS (3.8 L)

3 quarts (2.8 L) water

1 pound (455 g) carrots

4 stalks celery

2 onions

½ pound (225 g) mushrooms

1 red bell pepper

4 garlic cloves, sliced

3 bay leaves

1 teaspoon dried thyme

12 whole black peppercorns

½ pound (225 g) shallots (optional)

Other herbs as desired for more flavor

Chop vegetables (can be larger pieces).

In a large stainless steel or enamel pot, combine all ingredients. Bring to a boil and then reduce heat and simmer for 2½ hours. Uncover and continue to simmer for an additional hour.

Strain stock through a colander or sieve lined with cheesecloth.

Let cool and skim fat.

Return stock to a boil.

Ladle stock into hot jars. Leave a 1-inch (2.5 cm) headspace.

Remove any air bubbles. Wipe rims and secure lids.

Process pints (473 ml) for 30 minutes or quarts (946 ml) for 35 minutes at pressure listed for your altitude and canner (see Adjust for Altitude! on page 20).

Use a jar lifter to remove the jars place them on a clean dish towel away from any drafts. Let cool undisturbed for 12 to 24 hours and then check the seals. Store any unsealed jars in the refrigerator and consume within 2 weeks. Label the remaining jars with the recipe name and date before storing.

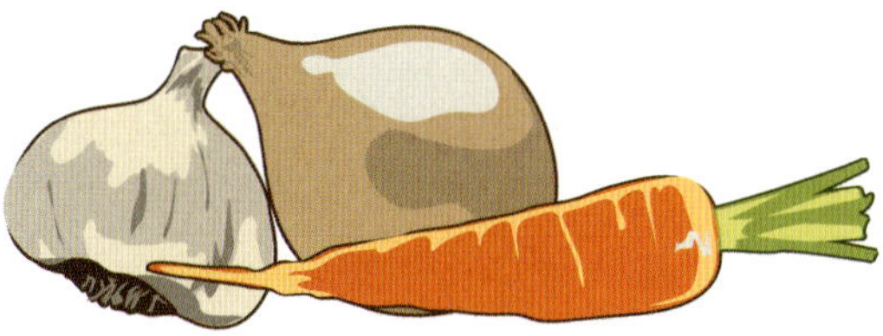

Chicken or Turkey Broth

Both chicken and turkey soup are frequent menu items on our farm. Yet, I make this broth quite often because it's so useful beyond just the expected soups. A cup of broth with a pinch of cayenne pepper soothes even the worst cold. And my college-age children always ask for jars of it take back to their dorm rooms. I'm sure it ends up the base of many quick and easy dinners! Make your turkey broth after the holidays and get the most out of the bird—truly using every bit of it. For this recipe, make the broth the day before you can it so you can chill it and skim off the fat. You can use a 10 to 15 pound (4.5 to 6.8 kg) carcass for this or you can use cuts with meat. Just remove the meat and use it for something else after cooking instead of canning it.

METHOD: PRESSURE CANNING

PROCESSING TIME: 20 MINUTES

PRESSURE:
10 POUNDS (68.9 KPA)
WEIGHTED GAUGE
11 POUNDS (75.8 KPA)
DIAL GAUGE

YIELD: 8 PINTS (3.8 L)

3 pounds (1.4 kg) chicken or turkey pieces

1 gallon (3.8 L) water

2 celery stalks

2 onions, halved, skin on

15 whole black peppercorns

3 whole bay leaves

Salt to taste

In a large stockpot over high heat, combine the poultry pieces and water. Bring to a boil.

Add the celery, onions, peppercorns, bay leaves, and salt. Reduce the heat to low and simmer, covered, for 2 hours, stirring occasionally.

Strain the hot broth through a cheesecloth-lined colander or fine-mesh sieve. Chill overnight.

The next day, remove and discard the fat layer on top before proceeding with the recipe. Reheat the broth to boiling.

Carefully ladle the hot broth into hot, sterilized jars, leaving 1 inch (2.5 cm) of headspace.

Remove any air bubbles with a plastic or wooden utensil, adding more hot broth as needed to maintain the proper 1-inch (2.5 cm) headspace.

Wipe the rims and seal the jars hand-tight with the 2-piece lids.

Carefully transfer the filled jars to the rack inside the pressure canner. Process the jars at the pressure listed above for 20 minutes.

Let the canner return to 0 pounds pressure (0.7 kPa). Wait 10 minutes more and then carefully open the canner lid according to the manufacturer's instructions.

With a jar lifter, remove the jars and place them on a clean dish towel away from any drafts. Allow to cool undisturbed for 12 to 24 hours and then check the seals. If any jars have not sealed properly, refrigerate them and use the broth within 1 week. Label the remaining jars with the recipe name and date before storing.

Beef Bone Broth

Beef broth is perfect for those cold winter meals. It's a delicious treat on its own in a mug (just salt to taste) and is the ideal base for your favorite stew. Rather than shop for this recipe, I try to save all my beef bones in the freezer until I have enough for a batch of stock. The good news is, no bones are better than others for this recipe—save all of them! Be sure to remove any visible fat before freezing and store them in an airtight freezer bag. For this recipe, make the broth the day before you want to can it so you can chill it and skim off the fat. If you have a couple of days and a slow cooker, this recipe can be made that way as well. The flavor develops beautifully if cooked overnight.

METHOD: PRESSURE CANNING

PROCESSING TIME: 25 MINUTES

PRESSURE:
10 POUNDS (68.9 KPA)
WEIGHTED GAUGE
11 POUNDS (75.8 KPA)
DIAL GAUGE

YIELD: 8 PINTS (3.8 L)

3 pounds (1.4 kg) assorted beef bones

1 gallon (3.8 L) cold water

1 large yellow onion, halved, skin on

2 garlic cloves

Salt and ground black pepper to taste (optional)

In a large stockpot over high heat, combine the bones, cold water, onion, and garlic. Bring to a boil. Reduce the heat to low, cover the pot, and simmer for 4 hours. Alternatively, place all ingredients in a slow cooker set on low heat, cover the cooker, and cook for at least 8 hours or overnight.

Strain the broth through a cheesecloth-lined colander or fine-mesh sieve. Taste and season with salt or black pepper, if desired. Chill overnight.

The next day, remove and discard the fat layer on top before proceeding with the recipe. Reheat the broth to boiling.

Carefully ladle the hot broth into hot, sterilized jars, leaving 1 inch (2.5 cm) of headspace.

Remove any air bubbles with a plastic or wooden utensil, adding liquid as needed to maintain the proper 1-inch (2.5 cm) headspace.

Wipe the rims and seal the jars hand-tight with the 2-piece lids.

Carefully transfer the filled jars to the rack inside the pressure canner. Process the jars at the pressure listed above for 25 minutes.

Let the canner return to 0 pounds pressure (0.7 kPa). Wait 10 minutes more and then carefully open the canner lid according to the manufacturer's instructions.

With a jar lifter, remove the jars and place them on a clean dish towel away from any drafts. Allow to cool undisturbed for 12 to 24 hours and then check the seals. If any jars have not sealed properly, refrigerate them and use the broth within 1 week. Label the remaining jars with the recipe name and date before storing.

Garlic Broth

Broth is perhaps not the most glamorous of foods to can, but it is one of the nicest things to have on the shelf. Garlic broth is my little secret for restorative dishes. My favorite thing to do for a sick family member is to serve a mug of this with a few red pepper flakes floating in it. However, you can also use it in many recipes in place of Chicken or Turkey Broth (page 84). It's a great way to make your vegetable soups vegan without sacrificing the deep flavors that meat-based broths bring to a recipe.

METHOD: PRESSURE CANNING

PROCESSING TIME: 20 MINUTES

PRESSURE:
10 POUNDS (68.9 KPA)
WEIGHTED GAUGE
11 POUNDS (75.8 KPA)
DIAL GAUGE

YIELD: 8 PINTS (3.8 L)

20 garlic cloves, peeled

1 gallon (3.8 L) water

2 onions, halved, skin on

Salt and ground black pepper to taste

In a large stockpot over high heat, Combine the garlic and water. Bring to a boil.

Add the onions and reduce the heat to low. Simmer for 2 hours, stirring occasionally.

Carefully strain the hot broth through a cheesecloth-lined colander. Taste and season with salt and black pepper. Return the broth to the pot and heat over high heat until it boils. Turn off the heat.

Carefully ladle the hot broth into hot, sterilized jars, leaving 1 inch (2.5 cm) of headspace.

Remove any air bubbles with a plastic or wooden utensil, adding more hot broth as needed to maintain the proper 1-inch (2.5 cm) headspace.

Wipe the rims and seal the jars hand-tight with the 2-piece lids.

Carefully transfer the filled jars to the rack inside the pressure canner. Process the jars at the pressure listed above for 20 minutes.

Let the canner return to 0 pounds pressure (0.7 kPa). Wait 10 minutes more and then carefully open the canner lid according to the manufacturer's instructions.

With a jar lifter, remove the jars and place them on a clean dish towel away from any drafts. Allow to cool undisturbed for 12 to 24 hours and then check the seals. If any jars have not sealed properly, refrigerate them and use the broth within 1 week. Label the remaining jars with the recipe name and date before storing.

Vegetable Broth

The following vegetable broth recipe is my base—but it's a bit different each time I make it when it comes to the pound and a half (680 g) of vegetables. That's because, just as with the Beef Bone Broth (page 85), the base is built on extras that I stash away. I keep a freezer bag in my freezer to add to throughout the month. I throw in leftover vegetables, like half an onion, the tops of carrots, and occasionally, extras from the farmers' market. When that bag is full, I empty it in a stockpot and cover everything with water. This mix of vegetables makes a wonderful broth for many recipes. Naturally, this recipe should be the foundation of your next vegetable stew, but don't stop there. Use this broth for bean soups or try it in a recipe in place of chicken broth.

METHOD: PRESSURE CANNING

PROCESSING TIME: 20 MINUTES

PRESSURE:
10 POUNDS (68.9 KPA)
WEIGHTED GAUGE
11 POUNDS (75.8 KPA)
DIAL GAUGE

YIELD: 4 PINTS (1.9 L)

2 quarts (1.9 L) water

1½ pounds (680 g) assorted vegetables

2 large carrots, peeled and halved

1 celery stalk

1 onion, halved, skin on

2 garlic cloves

3 whole bay leaves

Salt and ground black pepper to taste

In a large stockpot over high heat, combine all the ingredients and season with salt and black pepper. Bring to a boil. Reduce the heat to low and simmer for 2 hours, stirring occasionally.

Carefully strain the hot broth through a cheesecloth-lined colander. Return the broth to the pot and heat over high heat until it boils. Turn off the heat.

Carefully ladle the hot broth into hot, sterilized jars, leaving 1 inch (2.5 cm) of headspace.

Remove any air bubbles with a plastic or wooden utensil, adding more hot broth as needed to maintain the proper 1-inch (2.5 cm) headspace.

Wipe the rims and seal the jars hand-tight with the 2-piece lids.

Carefully transfer the filled jars to the rack inside the pressure canner. Process the jars at the pressure listed above for 20 minutes.

Let the canner return to 0 pounds pressure (0.7 kPa). Wait 10 minutes more and then carefully open the canner lid according to the manufacturer's instructions.

With a jar lifter, remove the jars and place them on a clean dish towel away from any drafts. Allow to cool undisturbed for 12 to 24 hours and then check the seals. If any jars have not sealed properly, refrigerate them and use the broth within 1 week. Label the remaining jars with the recipe name and date before storing.

Kidney Bean Soup

Canned bean soups are a lot like canned beans—they can get the job done, but it's hard to get excited about them. Worse even, canned soups often pack lots of sodium—perhaps making up for their shortcomings in texture or flavor! This soup is a clear upgrade and, even better, kid approved. One of my family's favorite meals is a combination of this soup with fresh-from-the-oven biscuits. I've also done some testing and this recipe holds up just fine if you want to omit the ham and use vegetable broth instead of a meat-based broth. As far as the salt goes, I recommend canning this recipe as is and allowing your family (or guests) to season with salt and black pepper when serving. The salt in the broth may well be enough for some.

METHOD: PRESSURE CANNING

PROCESSING TIME: 1 HOUR

PRESSURE: 10 POUNDS (68.9 KPA) WEIGHTED GAUGE, 11 POUNDS (75.8 KPA) DIAL GAUGE

YIELD: 4 PINTS (1.9 L)

2 quarts (1.9 L) Chicken or Turkey Broth (page 84) or store-bought broth

1 cup (110 g) diced peeled potatoes

1 cup (154 g) fresh corn kernels

½ cup (50 g) sliced celery

½ large yellow onion, diced

1 garlic clove, thinly sliced

1 cup (150 g) cubed cooked ham

1 cup (256 g) canned and drained kidney beans

In a large stockpot over medium-high heat, combine the broth, potatoes, corn, celery, onion, and garlic. Cover the pot and heat until the mixture comes to a simmer.

Add the ham and kidney beans. Bring the mixture to a boil. Cook for 10 minutes.

Carefully ladle the hot soup into hot, sterilized jars, leaving 1 inch (2.5 cm) of headspace.

Wipe the rims and seal the jars hand-tight with the 2-piece lids.

Carefully transfer the filled jars to the rack inside the pressure canner. Process the jars at the pressure listed above for 1 hour.

Let the canner return to 0 pounds pressure (0.7 kPa). Wait 10 minutes more and then carefully open the canner lid according to the manufacturer's instructions.

With a jar lifter, remove the jars and place them on a clean dish towel away from any drafts. Allow to cool undisturbed for 12 to 24 hours and then check the seals. If any jars have not sealed properly, refrigerate them and use the soup within 2 weeks. Label the remaining jars with the recipe name and date before storing.

Vegetable Soup

It's a mystery to me why many children who avoid vegetables come dinnertime will eat a full bowl of vegetable soup. Who am I to argue? I'm always happy to find a way to make sure my kids eat the vegetables I put in front of them. This soup is a personal favorite. It's what I reach for to pack a thermos for lunch when I'm headed out for the day. It's hearty and filling on its own, but you can make it more of a meal with a thick slice of buttered bread. One important note: Make sure you use chickpeas or another bean that has been precooked—don't use dried beans in this recipe!

METHOD: PRESSURE CANNING

PROCESSING TIME: 1 HOUR

PRESSURE: 10 POUNDS (68.9 KPA) WEIGHTED GAUGE, 11 POUNDS (75.8 KPA) DIAL GAUGE

YIELD: 3 PINTS (1.4 L)

1 pint (473 ml) canned tomatoes

2 cups (475 ml) water

1 cup (164 g) canned corn

1 cup (240 g) canned and drained chickpeas, or other cooked bean

3 carrots, sliced

1½ pounds (680 g) potatoes, peeled and cubed

1 medium-size onion, chopped

½ cup (50 g) chopped celery

2 garlic cloves, minced

Salt and ground black pepper to taste

1 teaspoon dried Italian seasoning

In a large heavy stockpot over high heat, combine the tomatoes, water, corn, chickpeas, carrots, potatoes, onion, celery, and garlic. Season with salt and black pepper. Stir to combine and bring to a boil. Reduce the heat to a simmer and stir in the Italian seasoning. Simmer the soup for 10 minutes.

Increase the heat and bring the soup to a boil again.

Carefully ladle the hot soup into hot, sterilized jars, leaving 1 inch (2.5 cm) of headspace.

Remove any air bubbles with a plastic or wooden utensil, adding more hot soup as needed to maintain the proper 1-inch (2.5 cm) headspace.

Wipe the rims and seal the jars hand-tight with the 2-piece lids.

Carefully transfer the filled jars to the rack inside the pressure canner. Process the jars at the pressure listed above for 1 hour.

Let the canner return to 0 pounds pressure (0.7 kPa). Wait 10 minutes more and then carefully open the canner lid according to the manufacturer's instructions.

With a jar lifter, remove the jars and place them on a clean dish towel away from any drafts. Allow to cool undisturbed for 12 to 24 hours and then check the seals. If any jars have not sealed properly, refrigerate them and use the soup within 2 weeks. Label the remaining jars with the recipe name and date before storing.

Thanksgiving Turkey Soup

This soup tastes like Thanksgiving in a jar. I often use the turkey bones from the big day to make the broth and throw in a little of the leftover turkey from our meal. Since I brine my turkey the night before, the meat starts out moist. I experimented by adding the cranberries one year and now I do it every time. Try it and you'll see—they seem to pull the whole recipe together.

METHOD: PRESSURE CANNING

PROCESSING TIME: 1 HOUR

PRESSURE:
10 POUNDS (68.9 KPA)
WEIGHTED GAUGE
11 POUNDS (75.8 KPA)
DIAL GAUGE

YIELD: 4 PINTS (1.9 L)

2 quarts (1.9 L) Chicken or Turkey Broth (page 84), or store-bought broth

½ cup (50 g) sliced celery

½ cup (61 g) sliced carrot

½ large yellow onion, chopped

1 cup (154 g) fresh or (164 g) canned and drained corn

½ cup (55 g) chopped fresh cranberries

1 cup (140 g) shredded cooked turkey

1 cup (177 g) Great Northern beans, cooked and drained

1 fresh sage leaf, or ½ teaspoon dried sage

Salt and ground black pepper to taste

In a large stockpot over medium-high heat, combine the broth, celery, carrot, onion, corn, and cranberries. Cover the pot and bring to a simmer.

Add the turkey, beans, and sage. Season with salt and black pepper. Continue cooking until the soup comes to a boil.

Carefully ladle the hot soup into hot, sterilized jars, leaving 1 inch (2.5 cm) of headspace.

Remove any air bubbles with a plastic or wooden utensil, adding more hot soup as needed to maintain the proper 1-inch (2.5 cm) headspace.

Wipe the rims and seal the jars hand-tight with the 2-piece lids.

Carefully transfer the filled jars to the rack inside the pressure canner. Process the jars at the pressure listed above for 1 hour.

Let the canner return to 0 pounds pressure (0.7 kPa). Wait 10 minutes more and then carefully open the canner lid according to the manufacturer's instructions.

With a jar lifter, remove the jars and place them on a clean dish towel away from any drafts. Allow to cool undisturbed for 12 to 24 hours and then check the seals. If any jars have not sealed properly, refrigerate them and use the soup within 1 week. Label the remaining jars with the recipe name and date before storing.

PRESSURE CANNING SOUPS

There is nothing like a comforting bowl of soup after a long day at work, as the perfect lunch, or when you don't feel well. Like most foods, home-canned soups taste better than store-bought cans—and you can leave out the questionable preservatives.

Making soups for canning is almost the same as making them to serve immediately for dinner. There are just a few simple rules to follow to be sure your soups are canned safely.

1. Do not add starches such as noodles and rice to your canned soups. These foods become mushy and fall apart during the canning process. Even if the soups look good after the jars come out of the canner, reheating the soup will result in a breakdown of the starches and an undesirable mushy texture. Add the rice or noodles to the soup after you crack the jar to serve it.
2. When canning soups, add more broth than you would when making it on the stovetop. I fill my jars one-fourth of the way with vegetables and meat and the rest of the way with broth.
3. Cooled soup may thicken slightly in the jar when using homemade meat broths. If this happens, it's completely normal. Once you reheat the soup, it will quickly thin again.
4. Some ingredients do not belong in canned soups as they become so strong in flavor they overwhelm the recipe—broccoli, cabbage, and brussels sprouts all taste too intense after canning, in my opinion. If you want to experiment with these ingredients, use less than you normally would so they don't overpower your recipe.
5. When adding dried beans to your soups, cook them before adding to the recipe. Dry beans absorb quite a bit of moisture and will absorb too much broth.

Mexican Chicken Soup

Slightly spicy, this soup is just right with a piece of fresh cornbread. I love serving it with a dollop of sour cream as well. Make it as spicy as you like. My family falls into the "medium heat" category, but the base recipe here is as mild as the taco seasoning you use. To spice it up, leave in some or all of the jalapeño seeds and add a few dashes of hot sauce when serving.

METHOD: PRESSURE CANNING

PROCESSING TIME: 1 HOUR

PRESSURE:
10 POUNDS (68.9 KPA)
WEIGHTED GAUGE
11 POUNDS (75.8 KPA)
DIAL GAUGE

YIELD: 4 PINTS (1.9 L)

2 quarts (1.9 L) Chicken or Turkey Broth (page 84), or store-bought broth

½ cup (50 g) sliced celery

½ large yellow onion, chopped

2 garlic cloves, sliced

1 cup (180 g) diced tomatoes

1 cup (154 g) fresh or (164 g) canned and drained corn

1 jalapeño pepper, seeded and minced

1 cup (140 g) shredded cooked chicken

1 cup (240 g) canned and drained black beans

2 teaspoons taco seasoning

Salt to taste

In a large stockpot over medium-high heat, combine the broth, celery, onion, garlic, tomatoes, corn, and jalapeño. Cover the pot and bring to a simmer.

Stir in the chicken, black beans, and taco seasoning. Taste and add salt, if desired. Continue to heat the broth to a boil.

Carefully ladle the hot soup into hot, sterilized jars, leaving 1 inch (2.5 cm) of headspace.

Remove any air bubbles with a plastic or wooden utensil, adding more hot soup as needed to maintain the proper 1-inch (2.5 cm) headspace.

Wipe the rims and seal the jars hand-tight with the 2-piece lids.

Carefully transfer the filled jars to the rack inside the pressure canner. Process the jars at the pressure listed above for 1 hour.

Let the canner return to 0 pounds pressure (0.7 kPa). Wait 10 minutes more and then carefully open the canner lid according to the manufacturer's instructions.

With a jar lifter, remove the jars and place them on a clean dish towel away from any drafts. Allow to cool undisturbed for 12 to 24 hours and then check the seals. If any jars have not sealed properly, refrigerate them and use the soup within 1 week. Label the remaining jars with the recipe name and date before storing.

Traditional Chicken Soup

METHOD: PRESSURE CANNING

PROCESSING TIME:
PINTS (473 ML) 75 MINUTES;
QUARTS (946 ML) 90 MINUTES

YIELD: 6 PINTS OR 3 QUARTS (2.8 L)

2 cups (280 g) diced chicken

3 quarts (2.8 L) chicken stock (see recipe for Chicken Stock on page 82)

2 stalks celery, diced

3 carrots, diced

1 large onion, diced

1 teaspoon dried tarragon (or other herb if preferred)

1 tablespoon (18 g) salt

1 teaspoon freshly ground black pepper

In a large stainless steel or enamel pot, combine all ingredients. Bring to a boil and then reduce heat and simmer for 30 minutes.

Ladle soup into hot, sterilized jars. Leave a 1-inch (2.5 cm) headspace.

Remove any air bubbles. Wipe rims and secure lids.

Process pints (473 ml) for 75 minutes or quarts (946 ml) for 90 minutes at pressure listed for your altitude and canner (see Adjust for Altitude! on page 20).

Use a jar lifter to remove the jars and let cool undisturbed on a clean dish towel away from any drafts. Check the seals after 12 to 24 hours. Refrigerate any unsealed jars and use within 2 weeks. Label the remaining jars with the recipe name and date before storing.

NOTE

Do NOT can chicken soup with noodles. When you're ready to eat chicken noodle soup, pour canned broth and vegetables into a pan and add the noodles. Cook until noodles are tender.

Lentil and Kielbasa Soup

This is a hearty meal in a bowl!

METHOD: PRESSURE CANNING

PROCESSING TIME: 90 MINUTES

YIELD: 5 QUARTS (4.7 L)

2½ cups (480 g) dried lentils, rinsed

1½ pounds (680 g) kielbasa (smoked sausage), sliced into ½-inch (1.3 cm) pieces

2 large onions, chopped

5 carrots, chopped

7 garlic cloves, chopped

6 pounds (2.7 kg) tomatoes, peeled, seeded, and chopped

¼ cup (5 g) dried parsley

1½ tablespoons (11 g) ground cumin

2½ tablespoons (18 g) paprika

1 tablespoon (18 g) salt

5 cups (1.2 L) chicken or vegetable stock

2 teaspoons ground black pepper

Add lentils and 8 cups (1.9 L) of water to a stockpot. Bring to a boil and boil for 2 minutes. Set aside to soak for an hour.

Drain lentils. Add 8 cups (1.9 L) of fresh water, return to a boil, and then strain, reserving lentil water. Transfer lentils to hot, sterilized quart jars (946 ml), filling each jar a quarter full.

Add remaining ingredients and lentil water to a stockpot and simmer for 15 minutes.

Divide vegetables and kielbasa into hot, sterilized jars. Top off with soup liquid, leaving a 1-inch (2.5 cm) headspace. If necessary, add additional boiling water to jars to fill.

Remove any air bubbles. Wipe rims and secure lids.

Process in a pressure canner for 90 minutes at pressure listed for your altitude and canner (see Adjust for Altitude! on page 20).

Use a jar lifter to remove the jars and let cool undisturbed on a clean dish towel away from any drafts. Check the seals after 12 to 24 hours. Refrigerate any unsealed jars and use within 2 weeks. Label the remaining jars with the recipe name and date before storing.

Masoor Dal Soup

METHOD: PRESSURE CANNING

PROCESSING TIME:
PINTS (473 ML) 75 MINUTES;
QUARTS (946 ML) 90 MINUTES

YIELD: 5 PINTS (2.4 L)

2½ cups (480 g) dried split red lentils

1 medium yellow onion, chopped

3 carrots, sliced

2 garlic cloves, minced

½ cup (120 ml) water

6 cups (1.4 L) chicken or vegetable stock

1 lemon, sliced and seeded

1 tablespoon (6 g) curry powder (Use a good quality.)

1 teaspoon freshly grated ginger

2 bay leaves

Add lentils and 8 cups (1.9 L) of water to a stockpot. Bring to a boil and boil for 2 minutes. Set aside to soak for an hour.

Drain lentils. Add 8 cups (1.9 L) of fresh water, return to a boil, and then strain, reserving lentil water. Transfer lentils to hot, quart-sized (946 ml) sterilized jars, filling each jar halfway.

Add onions, carrot, and garlic to stockpot with ½ cup (120 ml) of water. Cook for 3 minutes.

Add stock, 4 cups (946 ml) of reserved lentil water, lemon, and spices to pot. Bring to a boil. Cover, reduce heat, and cook for 15 minutes. Add tomatoes and cook for 5 minutes. Remove lemon slices and bay leaves.

Ladle soup broth over lentils in canning jars, leaving a 1-inch (2.5 cm) headspace.

Remove any air bubbles. Wipe rims and secure lids.

Process pints (473 ml) for 75 minutes and quarts (946 ml) for 90 minutes at pressure listed for your altitude and canner (see Adjust for Altitude! on page 20).

Use a jar lifter to remove the jars and let cool undisturbed on a clean dish towel away from any drafts. Check the seals after 12 to 24 hours. Refrigerate any unsealed jars and use within 2 weeks. Label the remaining jars with the recipe name and date before storing.

To serve, heat and garnish with fresh cilantro and a pinch of garam masala.

Tex-Mex Vegetarian Chili

METHOD: PRESSURE CANNING OR BOILING WATER BATH CANNING (VARIATION AT END OF RECIPE)

PROCESSING TIME:
PRESSURE CANNING:
PINTS (473 ML) 75 MINUTES;
QUARTS (946 ML)
90 MINUTES

BOILING WATER BATH CANNING:
PINTS (473 ML) 50 MINUTES

YIELD: 5 PINTS (2.4 L)

1 cup (184 g) dried kidney beans

4 cups (946 ml) water

2½ pounds (1.1 kg) tomatoes, halved

1 onion, quartered

3 garlic cloves

½ green bell pepper, chopped

¼ jalapeño pepper

1½ teaspoons ground cumin

2 teaspoons paprika

½ teaspoon dried thyme

½ teaspoon dried sage

1 teaspoon dried oregano

1 teaspoon hot sauce

5 tablespoons (75 ml) lemon juice

Boil kidney beans in 4 cups (946 ml) of water for 2 minutes. Remove from heat and let set for an hour or overnight. Rinse beans and simmer in 4 cups (946 ml) of fresh water for 30 minutes.

Arrange tomatoes, onion, garlic, green bell pepper, and jalapeño in one layer on baking sheet. Broil 2 inches (5 cm) from heat, turning frequently with tongs until skins start to char, about 10 to 15 minutes. Cool and remove skins and seeds from tomatoes and peppers.

Add roasted vegetables, spices, and hot sauce to a stockpot. Cook at a simmer for 10 minutes.

Divide beans evenly among hot, sterilized canning jars. Ladle vegetable mixture into jars, leaving a ½-inch (1.3 cm) headspace. Top each pint (473 ml) with a tablespoon (15 ml) of lemon juice.

Remove any air bubbles. Wipe rims and secure lids.

Process pints (473 ml) for 75 minutes or quarts (946 ml) for 90 minutes in a pressure canner, at pressure listed for your altitude and canner (see Adjust for Altitude! on page 20).

Use a jar lifter to remove the jars and let cool undisturbed on a clean dish towel away from any drafts. Check the seals after 12 to 24 hours. Refrigerate any unsealed jars and use within 2 weeks. Label the remaining jars with the recipe name and date before storing.

To serve, heat chili. Mix a teaspoon of cornmeal with a tablespoon (15 ml) of water. Stir mixture into a pint (473 ml) of chili. Serve topped with shredded cheese.

VARIATION

To can this recipe using the Boiling Water Bath Canning (see page 20), omit the beans and simply add canned or rehydrated beans when serving the chili. Process pints (473 ml) for 50 minutes, adjusting for altitude.